Divine Intervention:
Jesus or Jefferson?

Divine Intervention:
Jesus or Jefferson?

Stanley Kimmel Kesselman

Regency/Vision Press

Published in the United States by Regency/Vision Press, Inc., Los Angeles, California.

Regency/Vision Press, Inc.
4804 Laurel Canyon Blvd. #807
Valley Village, CA 91607
(818) 623-8631

ISBN 978-1481906005

First Edition

10 9 8 7 6 5 4 3 2 1

Library of Congress Cataloging-in-Publication Data on file with publisher.

Author's web: www.JesusOrJefferson.com

Cover Design: Patti Fisher
Book Design: Craig Hines

Printed in the United States of America

Table of Contents

Table of Contents . . .

Alphabetical Order of Cited Books of the Bible

Do not forsake wisdom, and she will protect you;
Love her, and she will watch over you.
(Proverbs 4:6)

Introduction

The quest—and even the prescription—for world peace and human goodness is an extraordinarily difficult one. God knows.

In the last century, more than one hundred million people perished from the wars, starvation, disease, and mayhem unleashed by a gallery of evil rogues. The list is a portrait in horror: Hitler, Stalin, Lenin, Mao, Pol Pot, Idi Amin, Mussolini, Hussein, Kim Jong, and *countless* others. We are right to wonder why Christianity, Islam, and Judaism provided scant assistance during the last century's monumental struggles between good and evil or, for that matter, during the horrific evils of the preceding two thousand years.

In this new century, brutal life-and-death struggles play out in the lands of Middle Eastern tribal cultures from whence scriptural monotheism first arose. In Iraq, Afghanistan, Israel/Palestine, and other nearby killing zones, the bloodletting in God's name and from evil's gun barrel continues. Terror for the sake of terror is in play. And tomorrow, the conflicts' proponents may spill rivers of blood in other neighborhoods as the world nervously anticipates the next catastrophe.

But wherever future terror is outsourced, it is a near certainty that the Near East's three ancient scriptures will fail in their original divine missions to restrain evil. Absent profound change, the world will experience again and again the trademark brutality of the ancient desert Bible belt.

The Hebrew Bible, New Testament, and Koran are hand-me-downs revealed to superstitious tribes millennia ago. Their world is not ours. Nevertheless, the three brother faiths still call us back in time to the same Father via three antiquated lines of communication. Judaism's text is three thousand years old, Christianity's approaches two thousand years, and baby brother Koran was delivered to the Muslims fourteen centuries ago. The truths of centuries past—if they ever worked—are broken swords in the modern struggles against evil and for liberty. Consider these truths of the ancient Near East:

> *If two men are having a fight, and the wife of one tries to help her husband by grabbing hold of the other man's genitals, show her no mercy; cut off her hand. (Deut. 25:11–12 Old Testament)*

> *Everyone must obey state authorities, because no authority exists without God's permission, and God has put the existing authorities there. Whoever opposes the existing authority opposes what God has ordered. (Rom. 13:1–2 New Testament)*

> *Allah has promised the . . . unbelievers the fire of hell to abide therein; it is enough for them, and Allah has cursed them and they shall have lasting punishment. (Koran 9.68)*

So it was in those ancient times when most people still worshipped idols and child sacrifice was not uncommon. Today this book offers a new and hopeful way. The Final Testament. It is liberty as the faith that was delivered by America's divinely inspired Founding Fathers. It is a dramatic and powerful new course that traditionally faithful and independent truth seekers will find inspirational.

It is the last best chance for a peaceful world.

.ﻭ .ﻭ .ﻭ .ﻭ .ﻭ

We know how man's story began at the dawn of time in the biblical garden of Eden. Had we been present, our voice of collective experience would have implored, "No, Eve, no, don't do it. Don't listen to the evil snake. *Please . . . no . . . don't!*"

But there were no such words of caution for the young naïf, naked in mind and body. Such complete innocence swims without the life jacket of worldly restraint. So the worst occurred—Eve plucked the forbidden fruit from the Tree of Knowledge, and for 5,768 years thereafter (according to the Hebrew calendar), God has struggled to subdue the resulting evil.

The battle has been maddening. Not long after the Garden of Eden became a dangerous neighborhood, the ancient Lord grew despondent, and when he

> *saw how wicked everyone on earth was and how evil their thoughts were all the time, he was sorry that he had ever made them and put them on earth. (Gen. 6:5–6)*

What's an ancient God to do? First, the unimaginable—annihilation:

> *I will wipe out these people I have created, and also the animals and the birds, because I am sorry that I made any of them. (Gen. 6:6–7)*

Save for Noah, his family, and their animal pairs who sailed a huge ark through the great flood, the Lord's execution proceeded:

> *Every living being on the earth died—every bird, every animal, and every person. Everything on earth that breathed died. (Gen. 7:21–22)*

God soon realized his mistake: that as long as even one man lived, evil would continue. While the horrific cataclysm wrought by forty days of biblical downpour drowned mankind, hydra-headed evil swam to safety. Evil survived. Thus, the intended remedial prescription of a flood holocaust had been a divine error of incalculable dimension. So the Lord said, "Never again."

> *Never again will I put the earth under a curse because of what people do. I know that from the time they are young their thoughts are evil. . . . I promise that never again will all living things be destroyed by a flood. (Gen. 8:21, 9:15)*

Tragically, in that first great confrontation between God and Satan, mankind lost. Evil continued. However, God was ready to try again, and the second effort is recorded in the Old Testament

(Hebrew Bible). For its day—about three thousand years ago—it was a uniquely progressive strategy. Instead of drowning evil beneath a flood of water, he would destroy it with a flood of statutes. Thus, from Mount Sinai in the Egyptian desert, the Lord decreed a tablet of ten famous commandments—along with six hundred lesser-known others—to form a complete body of laws for holy living. Evil would be legislated out of existence:

> *Condemn to death anyone who offers sacrifices to any God except me, the Lord. (Exod. 22:20)*

> *If a man has sexual relations with another man, they have done a disgusting thing, and both shall be put to death. (Lev. 20:13)*

> *Whoever curses his father or his mother is to be put to death. (Exod. 21:17)*

> *Do not mistreat any widow or orphan. If you do, I the Lord . . . will become angry and kill you in war. Your wives will become widows, and your children will be fatherless. (Exod. 22:22–24)*

The Lord dramatically field-tested his new anti-evil weapon in the Sinai Desert and then in ancient Canaan (now Israel). Twelve Hebrew tribes were chosen to receive and live according to the stringent demands of divine law. They tried. They failed. Sheriff God was often brutal in enforcing the law, but in the end, evil was still everywhere.

Then the Hebrew Bible ends with the announced coming of the end. Evil was winning, and a new cataclysm would wipe the slate clean; but it never happened.

So what's a God to do? Try again? Jesus was born, and there began yet another cycle of divine war against an invigorated Satan. The epic battle of good versus evil was again fought in the parched barrio known as Canaan. But was it really *divine*? Was a creed of loving pacifism the Lord's ultimate weapon against virulent malevolence? Christianity offered vague hope against evil in *this* world while emphasizing the grand prize of salvation in the *next*. Under a strategy of love and retreat in the earthly battle against Satan, the army of Christian faithful was to reassemble in a heavenly dimension, but until the coming apocalypse

> *love your neighbor as you love yourself. If you love others,*
> *you will never do them wrong; to love, then, is to obey the*
> *whole law. (Rom. 13:10)*
>
> *Love your enemies and pray for those who persecute you,*
> *so that you may become the children of your Father in heaven.*
> *(Matt. 5:43–45)*

Were these New Testament revelations the Lord's sharpest spears against evil? "Of course," goes the response of the Christian faithful, but are they right? We shall see.

Jesus and his apostles preached that the end was very near. God had had enough of Satan and earthly battles against him. The good news was that the formula of faith in Jesus for the reward of eternal salvation was available to all. Heaven was wide open for business. The bad news? Eternal damnation was the price for refusing the offer—or for never receiving it.

Whether divine or merely inspired, Christianity was a new declaration of war against evil with a promised victory lap in an unseen heaven, not on earth. *Divine intervention?* In any event, goodness remained a rare oasis in the Bible belt.

So what's a God to do? Try again? Islam asserted that the Lord (pronounced *Allah* in Arabic) finally got it right centuries later. Detailed new war plans in the fight against Satan were angelically delivered in secret to the Prophet Muhammad during the years AD 610–630: it was the Koran. That complex scripture offered much that was progressive in its time, especially in its place—the same rough Near East neighborhood which had been the devil's playground since the beginning of time. Nevertheless, the question needs to be asked, has Islam slain the beast? Ironically, many now argue that Islam *is* the beast.

What did God do next? Apparently, not much for a least a

millennium after Muhammad. Then, in 1776, the world changed when these words were written:

> *We hold these truths to be self-evident, that all men are cre-*
> *ated equal, that they are endowed by their Creator with certain*
> *unalienable Rights, that among them are Life, Liberty, and the*
> *pursuit of Happiness.*

Most people recognize these words as a passage from America's Declaration of Independence written by Thomas Jefferson and formally adopted on July 4, 1776. Usually unrecognized is that this Declaration, the Constitution of the United States with its Bill of Rights, and the essays known as "the Federalist Papers," completely revised mankind's relationship with God and with each other.

More than a revolution of war, Jefferson and his colleagues were inspired to author a revolution in rights. The divine right of kings gave way to the divine right of liberty. For the first time, man was viewed as a sovereign being to whom God gave broad freedoms and liberties that neither man nor nation may deny or diminish. In the eighteenth century, such ideas were as radical as anything Moses, Jesus, or Muhammad had ever offered their tribesmen.

Could it be that between 1776 and 1791 the desert's ancient scriptures were superseded by a new world's new covenant—*the final covenant*—one delivered not in secret but in sunlight to an astonished world? Or had God retired after giving a message to Muhammad, or even earlier? Are the faithful forever bound by ancient revelations ordering death for insolent sons, love for those who would kill you, and a heavenly paradise to martyrs for mayhem?

What better work has been done than the revolutionary spread of the most powerful idea in history: that the Creator endowed mankind with inalienable rights that, like our hearts and souls, are inseparable from our humanity? History provides no other act of God or man so profoundly good or valuable. Was this epochal change *divine intervention*?

When and through whom divine intervention has occurred in mankind's affairs is a matter of faith; the Bible shows that the Lord cannot or will not assure the victory of goodness. He needs or wants help, but whose help? Moses? Jesus? Muhammad? Thomas Jefferson? James Madison? As new truths emerge, faith can change. It has in the past, and it ought to today. This book's purpose is to precipitate a worldwide revolution in faith, leading to a peaceful world in which life, liberty, and the pursuit of happiness are universally experienced. The idea capable of moving the world is this: the Final Testament has arrived but remains unrecognized. A miracle *has* occurred. The uplifting power of the American Revelation has already spread around the globe, arguably improving more lives more quickly than all prior scripture combined. By recognizing the miracle of our gift, an energized call for liberty can reach the world's darkest corners where dictators, totalitarians, and thugs wearing cotton robes or silk ties trample inalienable rights and instinctive hopes.

The modern world is an especially dangerous place. If we believe that God exists, then history must reflect his presence for good somewhere. Faith suggests a divine eighteenth-century gift incalculably better than the failed ways of the ancients. And understandably so. The authors and historical figures of the Bible and Koran confronted trials that differ greatly from the tribulations of the modern age. Thus,

no foreigner shall eat the Passover meal, but any slave that you have bought may eat if you circumcise him first. (Exod. 12:43–44)

So if your right eye causes you to sin, take it out and throw it away! (Matt. 5:29)

When you travel through the earth there is no blame on you if you shorten your prayers for fear the unbelievers may attack you: for the unbelievers are your open enemies. (Koran 4:101)

The Final Testament—the Declaration of Independence, along with the Constitution, and the Federalist Papers—offers far greater hope than ancient scripture in the endless post–Adam-and-Eve struggle to defeat mass evil. Not all at once, but once and for all. We need no longer repeat ineffective mantras from ancient tribesmen whom we would never invite to dinner. We need no longer pray blindly in the long shadow of the Near East. No doubt, many people quietly yearn to wash their hands of that Jurassic Park of biblical conflict. However, with enough faith, we can imagine even Eve's old Iraqi neighborhood a garden of peace.

This book steps inside the covers of the Holy Bible in order to attend the birth of evil and observe its rise to power. From one chaotic corner of a still flat earth, the Old Testament gave the Western World a living God and his sacred rules for fighting back. We then proceed to Christianity's dramatically amended good-versus-evil battle plan. Pillars of belief about an "all merciful" Lord may wobble, and our vision of an idealized Jesus may falter, but these realizations are necessary reality bumps on the road to a new beginning. Finally, this volume discusses a program for canonizing the Final Testament and then harnessing the extraordinary power of human liberty as faith.

Divine Intervention: Jesus or Jefferson is intended for all people, not solely those of faith. It seeks to challenge our imaginations and raise questions about life-changing matters we take for granted. It argues that no other commandment can stop mass evil—that no other scripture will prevent future Attilas, Hitlers, Stalins, boot-heeled tyrants, thugs, and crooks from tragically proving that history tragically repeats itself. It posits faith in mankind, whose invigorated congregational energies can wrestle mass evil to the ground. God and diplomats have failed at the task for at least 5,768 years; but a billion congregational voices inspired toward values-based liberty will succeed.

It is appropriate to note that your author is not a pretend gospeler but a retired business lawyer—serious, instinctively skeptical, and unattached to establishment religion. However, the goal of universal liberty amid the sustaining virtues outlined by

America's Founding Fathers is an irresistible magnet. Nothing else like it has worked since the Garden of Eden. We have been immeasurably blessed by living free in the land of Thomas Jefferson, George Washington, Benjamin Franklin, James Madison, and other inspired leaders. Because of them, we owe future generations the best of our vision. We can honor that obligation by opening our eyes to a new possibility: the sacredness of our eighteenth-century gifts.

No matter your present views, you are likely to be tested, shaken, and almost certainly changed by this important journey. Truth has that effect. So does faith. Whether it is considered truth or faith, the Final Testament holds that the freedoms to speak, write, worship, assemble, and elect leaders of our choosing for limited periods are not concessions from the powerful but *every human's divine right*. This book is dedicated to making this right every person's fate.

PART ONE

THE OLD
TESTAMENT
(Hebrew Bible)

Chapter One

In The Beginning

The Old Testament begins with the book of Genesis, an immensely powerful and poetic birthing of earth and universe in which our planet is but a speck:

> *In the beginning when God created the universe, the earth was formless and desolate. The raging ocean that covered everything was engulfed in total darkness, and the spirit of God was moving over the water. (Gen. 1:1–2)*

> *Then God commanded, Let there be a dome . . . and it was done. So God made a dome, and it separated the water under it from the water above it. He named the dome "Sky." (Gen. 1:6–8)*

Genesis introduces the breathless power of God while showing the limited context of the word: an all-knowing Lord is presenting his autobiography within the narrow boundaries of knowledge of ancient priests. It was believed in biblical times that a dome covered a flat earth, and God's word never reveals otherwise. The Bible refers to the four corners of the world because then it was believed to have four corners.

Yet the power of God is boundless in an incomprehensively large universe, all part of his creation in seven days. Perhaps the seven days is intended as metaphor; we cannot know because no human was present to witness or record the events. Nevertheless, the creation was God's work:

> *So God made the two larger lights, the sun to rule over the day and the moon to rule over the night; he also made*

the stars ... and God was pleased with what he saw.
(Gen. 1:16–18)

It is all beyond imagining. Consider that as imposing as Earth is, we exist on a minute pebble in the orbit of a sun star 1.3 million times the size of our planet, in a galaxy that is one of at least 120 *billion* galaxies in the vastness of endless space.

For most people, however, God's most miraculous invention is called Adam, a man molded from clay, a complex organism consisting of at least twenty-five *trillion* invisible cells, each containing more than twenty-five thousand impossibly complex genes. Such breathlessly remarkable creation is narrated in simple elegance:

> *Then the Lord God took some soil from the ground and formed a man out of it; he breathed life-giving breath into his nostrils and the man began to live. (Gen. 2:7)*

This living, breathing man is given a home in a place we imagine as paradise. However, it could not have been such, for within it was another of God's creations: evil. Why was there evil in the garden where God first put man? The Bible does not say, and readers rarely ask, but Adam and evil were contemporaries at the dawn of time in the first instance of life:

> *Then the Lord placed the man in the Garden of Eden to cultivate it and guard it. He told him, "You may eat the fruit of any tree in the garden, except the tree that gives knowledge of what is good and what is bad. You must not eat the fruit of that tree; if you do, you will die the same day." (Gen. 2:15–17)*

Thus, we learn that a swift death is the punishment for rule breaking.

God soon recognizes Adam's need for a companion and uses his unfathomable power to create a woman from one of Adam's ribs:

> *Then the Lord God made the man [Adam] fall into a deep sleep, and while he was sleeping, he took out one of the man's*

ribs and closed up the flesh. He formed a woman out of the rib
and brought her to him. . . . Woman is her name because she
was taken out of man. (Gen. 2:21–23)

Genesis then proceeds with the story of man's downfall, made possible by God's decision to allow the cunning snake to beguile his
naked, innocent children who had no experience of deception:

Now the snake was the most cunning animal that the Lord
God had made. The snake asked the woman, "Did God really
tell you not to eat the fruit from any tree in the Garden?" [Eve]:
"God told us not to eat the fruit of that tree [pointing] or even
touch it; if we do we will die." (Gen. 3:1–2)

The victimization of women is a strong biblical theme, beginning
in the garden with a devious snake intent on doing Eve harm. She
falls prey and then persuades Adam to share the apple, and, thus,
mankind gains knowledge of evil. Although God clearly has the
power to prevent the hapless woman from eating from the forbidden tree, he lets it happen. The "original sin," it could be said, was
casting Adam and Eve for failure in a play scripted and directed
by a divine author.

Things progressively grow worse. God, angered by the disobedience, punishes Eve with a vengeance:

And he said to the woman, "I will increase your trouble in
pregnancy and your pain in giving birth. In spite of this, you
will still have desire for your husband, yet you will be subject
to him." (Gen. 3:16)

As the first person on planet Earth, Adam is stunningly naïve.
Nevertheless, his punishment for the wrongdoing is a brutal life
sentence of hard labor:

[God] said to the man, "You listened to your wife and ate
the fruit which I told you not to eat. Because of what you have
done, the ground will be under a curse. You will have to work
hard all your life to make it produce enough food for you. It

*will produce weeds and thorns, and you will have to eat wild
plants. You will have to work hard and sweat to make the soil
produce anything."(Gen. 3:17–19)*

Adam's punishing labors continue for many years as he, according
to Genesis 5:4, lives to be 930 years old. His line of descendants
continues with Mahalalel living to be 895, Jared reaching 962,
and Methuselah setting the record at 969. Then God determines
that living so long is too good for the beings he observed and
makes a miraculous change by shortening the human life span:

*When people had spread all over the world . . . the Lord
said, "I will not allow people to live forever; they are mortal.
From now on they will live no longer than 120 years." (Gen.
6:1–3)*

Using his omnipotence, God is able to manipulate permanently
human genetic structure so that death arrives at least seven hundred years earlier than in the days of Adam and Eve. This miracle
of genetic reengineering displays again God's limitless power.
However, the question always persists, with such omnipotence,
why not defeat evil?

Although evil is on center stage from the Bible's outset, the
book of Genesis takes a more terrible turn as the punishment for
misbehavior is ratcheted up by a Lord seeing disgusting behavior everywhere. On a yet young earth, evil seems to have spilled
in all directions. Angry and vengeful, the Lord determines that
humankind's extermination is the answer:

*When the Lord saw how wicked everyone on earth was and
how evil their thoughts were all the time, he was sorry that he
had ever made them and put them on the earth. He was so filled
with regret that he said, "I will wipe out these people I have
created, and also the animals and the birds, because I am sorry
that I made any of them." (Gen. 6:5–7)*

All men, women, children, and most fauna are thus sentenced to
death, except Noah, a six-hundred-year-old man with "no faults

and the only good man of his time," along with his family and two of each kind of animal. The method of execution is slow and torturous, a combination of drowning and starvation resulting from forty days and nights of ceaseless downpour. On the fortieth day, the highest peak in the world was twenty-five feet below the flood's roiling surface:

> *Every living being on the earth died—every bird, every animal, and every person. Everything on earth that breathed died. (Gen. 7:21–22)*

Noah's family and their selected animals float to safety in the ark God had directed Noah to build. Then the Lord spoke to Noah, revealing perhaps the greatest irony ever:

> *Human beings were made like God, so whoever murders one of them will be killed by someone else. (Gen. 9:6)*

Only Noah's family can hear this stern injunction against murder because all other human beings had been murdered. On a planet twenty-five thousand miles around, only eight living souls and their paired animals remain to walk a tiny patch in Asia Minor while the rest of the earth lies lifeless and devastated. The cataclysm is so horrific that even God is shocked by what he has done. So he announces to Noah the "never again" covenant:

> *Never again will I put the earth under a curse because of what people do; I know that from the time they are young their thoughts are evil. . . . I promise that never again will all living beings be destroyed by a flood. (Gen. 8:21, 9:15)*

Thus, the story of the flood has an even greater dimension of tragedy because the holocaust was useless. God's execution of all the men, women, and children was for naught: people had been evil before the flood, and afterward, they would be so again.

Still another irony: the evil mankind to flourish after the flood would derive from Noah, who "had no faults and was the only good man of his time." Thus, evil would claw its way back from Noah's good set of genes. Why not again reprogram human biology and do away with evil once and for all? Surely, Noah's family—the only remaining souls on a post-flood planet—would have been willing subjects. All future history lay in the balance. Yet all future history shows the Lord passed on the opportunity to reprogram man's genetic structure to favor goodness.

After the flood, all the nations of the earth descend from Noah's sons: Shem, Ham, and Japheth (Gen. 10:1). The Bible records at length the family lines and tribes that they and their descendants produced. Shem, the oldest of Noah's boys, who lived to be six hundred—well beyond the godly limit of 120 years— produced his first child at age one hundred, just two years after the flood (Gen. 10:21). This son, Arpachshad, begat Shelah, who begat Eber, who begat Peleg, who begat Reu, who begat Serug, who begat Nahor, who begat Terah, who—two hundred and ninety two years after the flood—begat Abram (Gen. 11:10–26).

Abram became the biblical prophet Abraham, and the world was never the same.

Chapter Two

A braham—the biblical patriarch of Judaism, Christianity, and Islam—was born in the Babylonian city of Ur in what is now southern Iraq. The year is guessed to be about 2,000 BC. From Ur, the family moved with their slaves to Haran (northern Iraq). The Bible tells us nothing further of Abraham's origins-whether he was a good man like Noah, his occupation, the kinds of pagan gods he worshipped, or any hint as to why he among all others was called to greatness. Abraham the man remains as blank as the ancient Near East desert from whence he came.

Nevertheless, it was a remarkable event in religious history when God selected Abraham to be his partner and Abraham's descendants to be the chosen people. It was only Abraham to whom God spoke these fateful words:

> *Leave your country . . . and go to a land I am going to show you. I will give you many descendants, and they will become a great nation. (Gen. 12:1–2)*

Though seventy-five years old at the time, Abraham accepted the offer and moved his family and many slaves to Canaan (now Israel), which the Lord identified as the Promised Land. There, and later in Egypt and other nearby lands, Abraham's storybook life was a divine weaving of a bizarre and powerful adventure.

Western religious history begins with Abraham, the patriarch. It is he and the Lord who enter a covenant together, thereby, giving first life to the concept of a single invisible Almighty God. Abraham's era is the late Iron Age, more than a thousand years before the rise of Greek civilization. It is a time of wandering tribes, ignorance, and desert winds blowing strange ideas from one corner of the Near East to the other. It was so early in time that the camel had not yet been ridden by tribesmen, and the donkey was a prosperous man's chariot. Abraham was among the few who were prosperous; his worldly success was reflected in his many slaves and holdings in sheep and goats. Those were days when slavery was commonplace. Indeed, when Abraham's wife, Sarah, had not borne him any children, she suggests her slave as a surrogate:

> *The Lord has kept me from having children. Why don't you [Abraham] sleep with my slave? Perhaps she can have a child for me." (Gen. 16:2)*

Abraham did. They did, and the child's name was Ishmael. Islam records that the Muslims descended from Ishmael, and so their religion honors Abraham as their patriarch and the one God of Abraham as their Allah. The desert of millennia past was the common sand from which we all rose.

The epoch of the Near East ancients is wildly strange to even the most imaginative among us today. Abraham's journeys, always with God nearby, are a window into time unknown. So it was when Abraham and his wife moved to a land called Gerar where Abraham spread the word that Sarah was his sister because in that land the king took all the beautiful women for himself. Abraham feared the king would choose Sarah and "that they would kill me to get my wife" (Gen. 20:11). The king did take Sarah:

> *So King Abimelach of Gerar had Sarah brought to him. One night God appeared to him in a dream and said, "You are going to die because you have taken this woman; she is already married. (Gen. 20:2–3)*

However, Abimelach had not yet come near Sarah, and he pleaded for mercy, crying out that even Sarah had said she was Abraham's sister. God replied with a threat of vast slaughter that is a signature of the early Bible:

*[G]ive the woman back to her husband . . . But if you do not
give her back, I warn you that you are going to die, you and
all your people. (Gen. 20:7)*

You and all your people will die. God thus threatened genocide
in order to retrieve a wife publicly presented as a sister. For this
king, the choice was between obedience and total destruction. That
choice, repeatedly offered by God throughout the Hebrew epoch,
was often the introduction to incalculable devastation. Obedience
to God or death is the theme for much of the Old Testament.

The introduction to the one God precedes the formation of
a formal religion. It was a pagan world except for Abraham. No
Judaism, Christianity, or Islam—there was only God and Abraham,
partners in a new enterprise still without rules, laws, testaments,
rituals, revelations, or any notion of a heavenly paradise. There
was a highly activist God, menacingly tough, and willing to make
the threat that thousands of innocent women and children would
die as a collective punishment for their king's one transgression.

The flavor of these ancient times and of God's early character is repeatedly and colorfully revealed in the Bible in the many
stories about Abraham. On one occasion, Abraham seeks the
assurance that God is earnest in his commitment to give Abraham's future generations the land of Canaan. God is willing to
allay Abraham's concern but in doing so, the Lord requests the
scene be set appropriately for the giving of a divine reassurance.
With great attention to detail, God says:

*"Bring me a cow, a goat, and a ram, each of them three
years old, and a dove and a pigeon." Abram brought the animals to God, cut them in half, and placed the halves opposite
each other in two rows. (Gen. 15:9–10)*

God is satisfied with Abraham's sacrifices and renews the pledge
of a future kingdom. In similar ways throughout the Old Testament, God requests specific animal sacrifices and rituals. Later, it
is decreed by the Lord to be a capital offense not to follow such
instructions to the letter.

Chapter Three

To understand further the story of evil and God's efforts to tame it, we visit a man named Lot, Abraham's nephew who lived in the town of Sodom, next to Gomorrah in what is now thought to be either Iraq or Syria. God was angry with the inhabitants of the area because he suspected them of being evil. Not being entirely sure, he sent angels to investigate. When they arrived, Lot practiced the ancient tribal custom of welcoming strangers by inviting God's disguised agents to his home. Sodom and Gomorrah are often synonymous with evil:

> *When the two angels [sent by God but looking like men] came to Sodom that evening Lot . . . got up and went to meet them . . . and said, "Sirs, I am here to serve you. Please come to my house," and finally they went with him to his house. Before the guests went to bed, the men of Sodom surrounded the house. All the men of the city, both young and old were there. They called out to Lot and asked, "Where are the men who came to stay with you tonight? Bring them out to us!" The men of Sodom wanted to have sex with them. Lot went outside . . . and said to them, "Friends, I beg you, don't do such a wicked thing! Look, I have two daughters who are still virgins. Let me bring them out to you, and you can do whatever you want with them. But don't do anything to these men; they are guests in my house, and I must protect them." (Gen. 19:1–8)*

Lot was a favorite of God for protecting strangers even at the expense of his daughters and was therefore saved. Tribal custom was important; girls and women were not. As to the men of Sodom and the companion town of Gomorrah, their wickedness—along with the innocent people living there—was capitally punished en masse:

> *Suddenly the Lord rained burning sulfur on the cities of*
> *Sodom and Gomorrah and destroyed them . . . along with all*
> *the people there and everything that grew on the land. (Gen.*
> *19:24–25)*

God's fury survives as part of the Bible because in ancient times Sodom and Gomorrah's complete destruction was perceived as just. The value of hospitality to travelers over the worth of the family virgins was favored by God in his approval of Lot's conduct. However, homosexuality was a capital offense, and capital executions included the deaths of any innocents in the killing zone.

But God was not yet finished with Lot, who like his uncle Abraham, would be the father of a future kingdom. Fatherhood for Lot would arrive in a most bizarre way. His two virgin daughters, the ones earlier refused by Sodom's male sex-crazed mob, are distraught over the dim possibility of ever experiencing husbands or motherhood:

> *Our father is getting old, and there are no men in the whole*
> *world to marry us so that we can have children. (Gen. 19:31)*

Late at night, Lot is made drunk by his daughters who then rape him as he lies in a stupor. The resulting sons were the ancestors of the Moab and Ammonite nations of Canaan (Genesis 20:34–39), not an inconsiderable reward for rape and incest.

As we have seen, Abraham was a man of his own time in being willing to save himself by giving up his wife to the lusty king. However, he was also a man for all time in being seduced by glory; if not for himself, then at least for the generations to follow. The promise of kingdom in exchange for faith was the basis for the founding of monotheism, the belief in the one God:

> *I will keep my promise to you [Abraham] and your descen-*
> *dants . . . in an everlasting covenant. I will be your God and*
> *the God of your descendants. I will give to you and to your*
> *descendants this land in which you are now a foreigner. The*
> *whole land of Canaan will belong to your descendants forever,*
> *and I will be their God. (Gen. 17:7–8)*

Made perhaps four thousand years ago, this covenant is still central to the fighting and dying in modern-day Canaan/Israel. In fact, the promised territory was perhaps ten times the patch of land now occupied by Israel, which was described as

> *all this land from the border of Egypt to the Euphrates river.*
> *(Gen. 15:18)*

Nothing as golden as an eternal kingdom comes easily or without strings. First, Abraham's descendants were to endure centuries of cruel slavery before the gift of the Promised Land would be presented:

> *Your descendants [Abraham] will be strangers in a foreign*
> *land; they will be slaves there and will be treated cruelly for*
> *four hundred years. (Gen. 15:13)*

Cruel slavery for four hundred years in Egypt. For many, it was a fate worse than death. To be treated "cruelly" in biblical terms is to suffer far beyond our modern comprehension. Abraham's circle probably then consisted of fewer than fifty people plus his goats and sheep. Was it merciful to punish everyone? Although, Abraham himself was not to endure slavery, God had a further stipulation that would touch Abraham quite personally:

> *You [Abraham] and your descendants must all agree to cir-*
> *cumcise every male . . . including slaves. Each one must be*
> *circumcised, and this will be a physical sign to show that my*
> *covenant with you is everlasting. (Gen. 17:10–13)*

God's word records that that same day, during Abraham's ninety-ninth year, he sealed the covenant by circumcising his thirteen-year-old son; all the males in the household, including many slaves, and, it appears, himself. Thus, from his tent in a prehistoric time, in a land of herdsmen and camel traders, the covenant between God and his chosen people was painfully sealed in flesh cut from the tip of man's vulnerable trophy. In the Iron Age's era of dull blades and rough cuts, circumcision was surely a terrifying down payment on a Promised Land.

The Old Testament is perhaps history's richest collection of stories. The tales of incest, tragedy, murder, deceit, ravage, slaughter, and revenge flow endlessly throughout the biblical epoch. God was correct in noting the prevalence of mankind's evil acts, but those misdeeds were often overshadowed by the Lord's own sense of horrific justice. Occasionally, God merely watched and condoned the awful meting out of revenge in the name of justice.

So it was in the story of Abraham's great-granddaughter Dinah. Abraham had a son named Isaac and a grandson named Jacob—both deemed prophets in the Old Testament. Jacob's daughter Dinah was raped, and the story reflects the age we must understand in order to understand the Bible:

> *One day Dinah . . . went to visit some of the Canaanite women. When Shechem son of Hamor the Hivite, who was king of that region, saw her, he took her and raped her. But he found the young woman so attractive that he fell in love with her and tried to win her affection. He told his father, "I want you to get Dinah for me as my wife." (Gen. 34:1–4)*

The rapist's father, Hamor, went to the girl's father Jacob trying to arrange a marriage. Because Jacob and his tribe were foreigners in Canaan, the young man's father made a radically progressive proposal to try to win Dinah for his son:

> *My son Shechem has fallen in love with your daughter; please let him marry her. Let us make an agreement that there will be intermarriage between our people and yours. Then you may stay here in our country with us; you may live anywhere you wish, trade freely, and own property. (Gen. 34:8–10)*

Then Jacob's sons, who were enraged at what had been done to their sister Dinah, took charge and made a deceitful deal, telling Shechem:

> *We can agree only on the condition that you become like us by circumcising all your males. (Gen. 34:15)*

Hamor, a wise leader who counseled his people toward acceptance of the foreigners, then put the circumcision proposal before
the Canaanite people in a public meeting. In perhaps the first
democratic vote in recorded history, all the Canaanite citizens
of the city agreed to the circumcision requested by the Hebrews.
Three days later, Jacob's sons wrought devastating revenge upon
the locals. They

> took their swords, went into the city without arousing sus-
> picion, and killed all the men, including Hamor and his son
> Shechem . . . After the slaughter Jacob's other sons looted
> the town to take revenge for their sister's disgrace. They took
> the flocks, the cattle, the donkeys and everything else in the
> city and in the fields. They took everything of value, captured
> all the women and children, and carried off everything in the
> houses. (Gen. 34:25–29)

These were the ways of illiterate tribes whose culture, traditions, and taboos are so foreign to our values and sensibilities.
Yet, God continued to bless his prophet Jacob after this episode.
We observe that the Lord's only announced law to that date—if
you kill a man you shall in turn be killed by another—found no
application in this story. Jacob's family killed many. There is no
record of punishment, only approval.

Recall that God had informed Abraham that his descendants
would be cruelly enslaved in Egypt. And they were:

> [The] more the Egyptians oppressed the Israelites, the more
> they increased in number and the farther they spread through
> the land. The Egyptians . . . made their lives miserable by forc-
> ing them into cruel slavery . . . and they had no pity on them.
> (Exod. 1:12–14)

Angered at the undiminished strength of the Israelites, the Egyptian king issued a command whose murderous horror we cannot
imagine:

> Take every newborn Hebrew boy and throw him into the
> Nile, but let all the girls live. (Exod. 1:22)

The resulting slaughter was ghastly. Perhaps thousands of male babies were dragged from their tents or mud houses, their help-less parents wailing and screaming out to God for help, as the king's soldiers pushed the children under the flowing waters of the Nile. God did nothing.

Many years later, the Hebrew plea to God for help was renewed. God agreed:

> *Years later the king of Egypt died, but the Israelites were still groaning under their slavery and cried out for help. Their cry went up to God, who heard their groaning and remembered his covenant with Abraham, Isaac, and Jacob. He saw the slavery of the Israelites and was concerned for them. (Exod. 2:23–25)*

Given God's limitless power, the task of liberation could have been easy. He could have sent the Egyptian king a dream commanding freedom for the slaves, and the deed would have been done.

Instead, God devises a scheme of punishments using Moses as his instrument. In general form, the story of Moses is well known, but the most revealing point in assessing the issues of justice and mercy in God's work is usually omitted from the telling: God elects to torture the Egyptian nation before freeing his people:

> *Now that you are going back to Egypt, be sure to perform before the king all the miracles which I have given you the power to do. But I will make the king stubborn, and he will not let the people go. (Exod. 4:21)*

God's plan was to "make the king stubborn" so he would not relent in favor of freedom. Moses, as God's instrument, turned the Nile River to blood. Pharaoh's divinely hardened heart pre-vented him from relenting. Then frogs filled the land, jumping into bedrooms, ovens, and baking pans. They were followed by gnats and flies that covered every inch of Egypt. The king was robbed of free will as his heart was divinely hardened, making him unable to give an order for freedom. Then, in a vast plague of death, every head of livestock belonging to the Egyptians died.

Next, hail, boils, locusts, and darkness engulfed the Egyptians, always leaving the Hebrews free of these horrors.

Always, with each horrific torture thrust upon the Egyptian nation, God's plan to devastate Egypt was in motion:

> [T]he Lord made the king stubborn and, just as the Lord had said, the king would not listen to Moses. (Exod. 9:12)

God was determined to show the king of Egypt again and again that he, the God of the Hebrews, was the most powerful of all the gods. Finally, enjoying the game for one last round, God told Moses:

> I will send only one more punishment on the king of Egypt and his people. After that he will let you leave. In fact, he will drive all of you out of here. (Exod. 11:1)

Moses was then instructed to repeat to the Egyptian king the following message from the Hebrew God:

> At about midnight I will go through Egypt, and every firstborn son in Egypt will die, from the king's son . . . to the son of the slave woman who grinds grain. The first born of all the cattle will die also. There will be loud crying all over Egypt, such as there has never been before or ever will be again. . . . Then you will know that I, the Lord, make a distinction between the Egyptians and the Israelites. (Exod. 11:4–7)

Moses gave this message to the king while God gave this unmerciful message to Moses:

> The king will continue to refuse to listen to you, in order that I may do more of my miracles in Egypt. (Exod. 11:9)

So it was. The king refused to listen, and God had the pleasure of performing another miracle of supreme destruction:

> At midnight the Lord killed all the firstborn sons in Egypt, from the king's son . . . to the son of the prisoner in the dungeon. . . . There was loud crying throughout Egypt, because

there was not one home in which there was not a dead son.
(Exod. 12:29–30)

No one knows the number, but surely, hundreds of thousands of people were tragically killed in this circus of death.

Only when the last miracle of death was completed did God permit the Egyptian king to relent and order Moses and his people to leave. However, before they began their journey, God demanded that another custom of that merciless epoch be carried out: the looting of the defeated. Pursuant to the Lord's instruction to take all the booty, the Israelites

> *asked the Egyptians for gold and silver jewelry and for clothes. The Lord made the Egyptians respect the [Hebrew] people and give them what they asked for. In this way the Israelites carried away the wealth of the Egyptians. (Exod. 12:35–36)*

After 430 years of slavery, the Hebrews left Egypt with great wealth, and according to tradition, much unleavened bread (Exod. 12:40). Their safe exit was then assured by the Lord's miraculous parting of the Red Sea.

The story of the exodus from Egypt—its timing, execution, and totality—is an example of divine power on display in great proportions. For all time, the story of the rescue from Egypt would be retold during the celebration of Passover, the holiday commemorating the death plague's passing over Hebrew homes as it took the lives of the Egyptian first born. The Lord as law-giver set the rules for holiday observance:

> *No foreigner shall eat the Passover meal, but any slave that you have bought may eat it if you circumcise him first. (Exod. 12:43–44)*

Today it would be unimaginable to have a slave at your holiday table, much less to surgically remove his foreskin before passing the traditional bitter herbs. The point here is not the dark humor, but rather the impenetrable distance between the biblical epoch and modern society. In order to see our way to the Final Testament, we must deeply experience the ancient ways of the old covenants. We must visit and understand the worlds of Moses and Jesus. We must try to wrap ourselves in the flavors, purposes, ignorance, harshness, and fears of ancient communities that would find much common ground with today's fundamentalist Islam. Shocking, perhaps, but that is the reality. We ache to have an all-merciful, all loving, and always-just God, despite a biblical record that is often painful to read because of God's violence toward humans and animals. To know this is not to despair but to be liberated, so that our hearts may be open to new and more optimistic truths. We shall see how the Final Testament is a liberating scripture suited to our times.

Returning to the ancient world, we find that the exodus from Egypt leads to the merging of a monotheistic, fundamentalist religious culture with patriarchal tribal customs. The setting is the rugged Sinai, where, following four hundred years of enslavement, the Hebrews are ready for hope and the Promised Land. Speaking through his prophet Moses, the Lord obliges this longing for a home, but as always, the ancient context of the Bible reflects an often unfathomable God. In this instance, he is one with a preference for donkeys and broken necks:

> *The lord will bring you into the land of the Canaanites, which he solemnly promised to you. . . . When he gives it to you, you must offer every firstborn male to the Lord. Every firstborn male of your animals belongs to the Lord, but you must buy back from him every firstborn male donkey by offering a lamb in its place. If you do not want to buy back the donkey then break its neck. (Exod. 13:11–13)*

The Israelites trekked across the barren wastes of the Sinai under the Lord's constant supervision. They were going to the Promised Land. What they did not know was that the "gift" of an empire from the Nile to the Euphrates was not to be handed to them like so many goats at a wedding celebration. Instead, there would be hundreds of years of inconclusive wars. There was no "gift" of a Promised Land because the many tribes that had long lived there had no intention of leaving.

The story of a caravan of former slaves moving across Sinai and the delivery of the Ten Commandments is a popular chapter of the biblical ethos. However, the episode is also a building block of Western civilization due to the cultural role played by the Ten Commandments for more than three thousand years.

The tribes reached Mount Sinai sometime around the year 1,300 BC, by which time civilizations had been long established in Egypt, Babylonia, Persia, China, India, Crete, and other areas of the Near East. There were already large cities, significant cultural developments, and even some lengthy legal codes, such as the Hammurabi Code in Persia.

At Mount Sinai, Moses carried out much business with God in an effort to prepare the tribes for their introduction to their patron Lord. On the third day at Sinai, God's noisy appearance broke the calm of the desert expanse:

> *On the morning of the third day there was thunder and lightning, a thick cloud appeared on the mountain, and a very loud trumpet blast was heard. All the people in the camp trembled with fear. (Exod. 19:16)*

> *"[Moses], warn the people not to cross the boundary to come and look at me; if they do, many of them will die." When the people heard the thunder and the trumpet blast and saw the lightning and the smoking mountain, they trembled with fear and stood a long way off. They said to Moses, "If you speak to us we will listen; but we are afraid that if God speaks to us we will die." (Exod. 19:21; 20:18–19)*

It is a scene of incalculable wonder: robed tribesmen in the desert, trembling before God's thunderous appearance. The Lord of the Egyptian miracles and Red Sea parting has come to give the law to his chosen people. He hands down at least 603 rules in addition to those famously referred to as the Ten Commandments. The extensive code of laws regulated all aspects of life and included many strict requirements for ceremonies and offerings pleasing to the Lord:

> *Every day for all time to come, sacrifice on the altar two one-year-old lambs. Sacrifice one of the lambs in the morning and the other in the evening. With the first lamb offer two pounds of fine wheat flour mixed with one quart of pure olive oil. Pour out one quart of wine as an offering. Sacrifice the second lamb in the evening, and offer with it the same amounts of flour, olive oil, and wine as in the morning. This is a food offering to me, the Lord, and its odor pleases me. (Exod. 29:38–41)*

The opening words of this instruction in sacrifice are enormously important. Nearly 3,300 years ago God ordered daily sacrifices of lamb for himself, *every day for all time to come.*

The Old Testament remains even today the unamended holy scripture of the Jewish religion. However, contrary to their Lord's instruction and in concession to innumerable cultural changes across the millennia, today's Jews have altered, reinterpreted, or simply ignore most of these "unchangeable" religious laws. God delivered 613 laws—including the Ten Commandments—to tired, fearful, hungry tribes camping in the barren Sinai thirteen hundred years before Caesar ascended in Rome. On their way from slavery in a despotic empire to a new home, the Law, or Mosaic Code, was delivered as a complete legislative program. It was an ancient and often bizarre rigor when God commanded:

> *Bring the bull . . . [and] kill the bull there in my holy presence. . . . Take some of the bull's blood and with your finger put it on the projections of the altar. Then pour out the rest of the blood at the base of the altar. Next, take all the fat which covers the internal organs, the best part of the liver, and the two kidneys with the fat on them, and burn them on the altar as an offering to me. But burn the bull's flesh, its skin and its intestines outside the camp. (Exod. 29:10–14)*

In addition to the many required animal sacrifices, God's eternal laws came with a price. The Lord instructed Moses regarding the collection of "protection money" in the form of taxes:

> *When you take a census of the people of Israel, each man is to pay me [the Lord] a price for his life, so that no disaster will come on him while the census is being taken. Everyone included in the census must pay the required amount of money, weighed according to the official standard. Everyone must pay this as an offering to me. (Exod. 30:11–13)*

No one today would suggest that God requested protection money, yet the Old Testament requires it because all regulations were postulated forever. Like almost all the 613 revealed laws, it is ignored. Of course, if such a tax were to be collected, we know that the Lord prefers the flat tax to a graduated tax:

> *The rich man is not to pay more, nor the poor man less, when they pay this amount for their lives. (Exod. 30:15)*

God informed Moses that he would live with his chosen people. For that reason, a tent of presence was constructed as the Lord's residence. The detail is breathtaking. The furnishings of the Lord's home on earth were lavish, such as an intricately detailed lamp stand containing "decorative flowers including buds and petals . . . and . . . seventy-five pounds of pure gold" (Exod. 25:31–33, 39). When the tent was completed, God gave Moses the instructions for anointing the tent of presence with a perfumed extravaganza:

> *Take the finest spices, 12 pounds of liquid myrrh, 6 pounds of sweet-smelling cinnamon, 6 pounds of sweet-smelling cane, and 12 pounds of cassia, all weighed according to the official standard. Add one gallon of olive oil, and make a sacred anointing oil, mixed like perfume. Use it to anoint the tent of my presence. (Exod. 30:23–26)*

This odoriferous tent in the desert must have been a wonderful treat to the senses. In the vast, open, boundless Sinai, nearly one thousand years before the greatest days of Athens, a golden ornate tent of enormous intricacy arose. From within powerful smells combining ancient perfumes, cinnamon, and exotica from the East floated on the hot breezes. These pleasant scents might just barely cover the stench of the disemboweled bulls and slaughtered lambs being brought in and taken out. In this ancient campground, the Lord revealed his Ten Commandments and hundreds of other laws, all to be obeyed until the end of time.

What laws were these?

If a man marries a woman and her mother, all three shall be burned to death because of the disgraceful thing they have done. (Lev. 20:14)

If a man has sexual relations with an animal, he and the animal shall be put to death. If a woman tries to have sexual relations with an animal, she and the animal shall be put to death. (Lev. 20:15–16)

If a man has intercourse with his uncle's wife, he disgraces his uncle . . . and neither one will have children. (Lev. 20:20)

Most societies teach respect of the elderly, and the Bible conforms:

Show respect for old people and honor them. Reverently obey me: I am the Lord. (Lev. 19:32)

Parents are also subjects of reverence. In the case of the Old Testament, however, God's mandate of capital punishment for disrespectful children is perhaps without parallel:

Whoever hits his father or his mother is to be put to death. (Exod. 21:15)

Whoever curses his father or his mother is to be put to death. (Exod. 21:17)

Some rules may strike us as old-fashioned while still reflecting common sense:

> *If someone steals a cow or a sheep and kills it or sells it, he must pay five cows for one cow and four sheep for one sheep. (Exod. 22:1)*

On the other hand, there is rough justice for thievery:

> *He must pay for what he stole. If he owns nothing, he shall be sold as a slave to pay for what he has stolen. (Exod. 22:2–4)*

Justice and death are often partners:

> *Put to death any woman who practices magic. (Exod. 22:18)*

> *Condemn to death anyone who offers sacrifices to any God except to me, the Lord. (Exod. 22:20)*

> *Do not mistreat any widow or orphan. If you do, I, the Lord, will answer them when they cry out to me for help, and I will become angry and kill you in war. Your wives will become widows, and your children will be fatherless. (Exod. 22:22–24)*

A society's laws reflect its problems, and its solutions define its sense of justice. Both change over time. However, the problems of the ancient Hebrew tribes and the justice prescribed to solve them are the foundation of Judaism, a testament written in stone because an omniscient God decreed they can never change. In reality, the Mosaic Code is largely ignored today, and yet the original foundation of the faith does not crumble; instead it has been built upon.

The Final Testament is not about abolishing monotheism's long and revered history, but rather it represents a new structure, a new covenant, built on top of the old. By studying the foundation, we can learn from the foundation builders' mistakes and build a strong and hopeful structure for our era and centuries to come.

Chapter Four

Western monotheism is based on a series of covenants, or contracts, of faith. Key was Abraham's covenant in which the Lord chose the patriarch's descendants. They are the chosen:

> *Keep all my laws and commands, so that you will not be rejected by the land of Canaan, into which I am bringing you. Do not adopt the customs of the people who live there; I am driving out those pagans so that you can enter the land. They have disgusted me with all their evil practices. But I have promised you this rich and fertile land as your possession, and I will give it to you. I am the Lord your God, and I have set you apart from the other nations. . . . You shall be holy and belong only to me, because I am the Lord and I am holy. I have set you apart from the other nations so that you would belong to me alone. (Lev. 20:22–26)*

Thus, tribes recently freed are told of a new kind of servitude: they belong to the one God in a solemn pact of faith for land, chosenness for holiness. However, bondage, even when loving, is painful and requires enormous discipline to suppress revolt. The resulting friction appeared quickly. Moses had climbed Mount Sinai to meet with God and receive the laws. When his return was delayed, the still-undisciplined people vented their impatience and voided their commitment to the Lord, saying to Moses's brother Aaron:

> *"We do not know what has happened to this man Moses, who led us out of Egypt; so make us a God to lead us." Aaron said to them, "Take off the gold earrings which your wives, your sons, and your daughters are wearing, and bring them to me." He took the earrings, melted them, poured the gold into a mold, and made a gold bull-calf. (Exodus 32:1–4)*

They proclaimed the gold calf their new god. How quickly—and how much—the people forgot. Recall that the Lord had turned the Nile to blood; covered Egypt in frogs, boils, and locusts; killed all the animals and firstborn Egyptian children; parted the Red Sea; and appeared in fiery clouds before their very eyes. Then, while Moses was away only a few weeks consulting with this omnipotent Lord, the people molded a diminutive bull-god to replace the greatest proven miracle worker of all time. What a strange world it was.

God was furious, saying to Moses:

> [T]hey have made a bull-calf out of melted gold and have worshipped it and offered sacrifices to it. They are saying that this is their god. . . . I know how stubborn these people are. Now, don't try and stop me, I am angry with them, and I am going to destroy them. (Exod. 32:8–10)

Moses pleaded to God not to destroy his chosen, reminding the Lord of past promises made:

> "Remember the solemn promise you made to them to give them as many descendants as there are stars in the sky and to give their descendants all that land you promised would be their possession forever." So the Lord changed his mind. (Exod. 32:13–14)

It is often stated that God showed his mercy and love for the chosen in this act of changing his mind. It is impossible not to wonder, however, if a decision to relent from a promise to destroy an entire people may be called 'love.' Calling off a holocaust is scant concession to the notion of freedom of religion and hardly evidence of divine mercy.

Nevertheless, the Old Testament's remarkable exchanges between God and his chosen are the brush strokes in the portrait of prehistoric tribal life. Thus, God's continuing instructions regarding sacrifices that pleased him were thoroughly gruesome. They are barbaric to our modern sensibilities:

If you are offering a bird as a burnt offering, it must be a
dove or a pigeon. The priest shall present it at the altar, wring
its neck, and burn its head on the altar. Its blood shall be
drained out against the side of the altar. . . . He shall take hold
of its wings and tear its body open . . . and then burn it whole
on the altar. The odor of this food offering is pleasing to the
Lord. (Lev. 1:14–17)

Another tradition of ancient tribes was polygamy. King Solomon
had hundreds of wives as well as seven hundred concubines.
Most men had far fewer, but one could imagine the jealousy and
sexual tension in households where women greatly outnumbered
men and where sons were tempted by the harem-like atmosphere.
God was surely wise in commanding his people to avoid such
temptation:

Do not disgrace your father by having intercourse with any
of his other wives. (Lev. 18:8)

Despite laws so anachronistic to a modern reader, the Hebrew
Bible also contains important principles of morality among its
613 statutes:

Do not steal or cheat or lie. Do not make a promise in [the
Lord's] name if you do not intend to keep it. (Lev. 19:11)

Do not rob or take advantage of anyone. (Lev. 19:13)

Do not hold back the wages of someone you have hired, not
even for one night. (Lev. 19:13)

Do not curse the deaf or put something in front of the blind
so as to make them stumble. (Lev. 19:14)

God's commands to his chosen people were to be taken seriously.
The Lord was a strict sheriff. Obey God's Law or else:

[Y]ou will serve the enemies that the Lord is going to send
against you. You will be hungry, thirsty, and naked—in need
of everything. The Lord will oppress you harshly until you

are destroyed. The Lord will bring against you a nation from the ends of the earth [and] they will swoop down on you like an eagle. They will be ruthless and show no mercy to anyone young or old. They will eat your livestock and your crops and you will starve to death. (Deut. 28:48–51)

In a sickening climax to the Lord's series of escalating threats for the crime of failing to obey, the beaten and tortured chosen will eat their own children in desperation:

When your enemies are besieging your towns, you will become so desperate for food that you will even eat the children that the Lord your God has given you. . . . Even the most refined woman of noble birth, so rich that she has never had to walk anywhere . . . will become so desperate for food that she will secretly eat her newborn child and the afterbirth as well. (Deut. 28:53–57)

If today a religious leader were to speak such words to his congregation, he would be called crazed and be removed at once.

"Thou shalt not murder" was carved in stone but ignored in life. Moreover, the all-knowing God—even as he threatens genocide for disobedience—already knows that his people *will in fact* disobey him. Thus, the horrific "eat your children" harangue is not just a threat but an actual sentence upon his people. This is what the Lord foresees as he talks to the prophet Moses:

You will soon die, and after your death the people will become unfaithful to me. . . . They will abandon me and worship the pagan gods of the land they are about to enter. When that happens, I will become angry with them; I will abandon them, and they will be destroyed. (Deut. 31:16–17)

The tribesmen of that early era, so God tells us, are going to abandon him and then be destroyed. It appears the unfaithful are pawns in a game of religious fate in which the moves to death have been predetermined. Perhaps these refugees from slavery heard whispers at the oasis or gossip over campfires that their God's threats against disloyalty would eventually doom their lives. Ordered to fear and believe, men, women, and children had no escape because it was their fate to die. They were unable to believe well enough or long enough.

God foresees the death of his people. He has the means to stop it because he is the executioner, but he refuses.

Chapter Five

S laves were commonplace in the biblical epoch. God does not approach the issue with twenty-first-century sensitivity. Rather, his word proceeds with matter-of-fact acceptance of an ancient Near East social norm. Indeed, slaves are twice referred to in the Ten Commandments:

> Observe the Sabbath and keep it holy. You have six days in which to do your work, but the seventh day is a day of rest dedicated to me. On that day no one is to work—neither you, your children, your slaves, your animals, nor the foreigners who live in your country.

> Do not desire another man's house; do not desire his wife, his slaves, his cattle, his donkeys, or anything else that he owns. (Exod. 20:9–10, 17)

Given the prominence of slavery, it is not surprising that several additional codes addressed the issue. God regulated everything and everyone with great specificity:

> Suppose a foreigner living with you becomes rich, while some Israelites become poor and sell themselves as slaves to that foreigner. . . . After they are sold they still have the right to be bought back . . . [by] a close relative . . . or they may buy their own freedom. . . . If they are not set free in any of these ways, they and their children must be set free in the Year of Restoration [every seventh year]. Israelites cannot be permanent slaves, because the people of Israel are the Lord's slaves. (Lev. 25:47–50, 54–55)

As one may expect, the bondage rules were considerably tougher for outsiders:

If you need slaves, you may buy them from the nations around you. You may also buy the children of the foreigners who are living among you . . . and you may leave them as an inheritance to your children, whom they must serve as long as they live. (Lev. 25:44–46)

In those dark days, parents sometimes sold their children into slavery or offered them for sacrifices on burning pyres. If we believe parents everywhere possess an instinctive need to love and keep their children, then we are forced to imagine the misery that would bring parents to such a breaking point. Perhaps it was at the point of starvation, when a child's sale would buy food to stave off death. Or perhaps a loving family would sell a starving child so he would survive on food from his slave master. In other instances, adults sold themselves into slavery, doing so in such numbers that God felt the need to regulate the practice. A choice favoring bondage suggests such a person's "free" life was so brutish, painful, and unpromising that slavery was the better alternative.

If we are unable to relate to so much that is ancient holy writ, would it not make sense for a maturing God to provide a fresh look at the fight against evil?

Faith suggests this occurred in AD 1776 as we shall later see.

Chapter Six

T he fourth book of the Bible, Numbers, tells of the Israelites' journey from Mount Sinai to the border of Canaan—the Promised Land—during a period of nearly forty years. It is called Numbers because the book begins with a detailed census, identifying each tribe and its leaders and showing the number of men fit for military service to be 603,550. God gave precise instructions as to how and where the groups were to camp and display their tribal banners.

Such strict governance is no guarantee of either good conduct or strong faith, and the parent-child relationship between God and his chosen was often tempestuous. Even for those tribe members who had survived slavery in Egypt, the rigors of life in Sinai were cause for complaining. And complain they did, too much and too often for God's taste. The Lord angrily reported to Moses that thousands of deaths would be the price for such faithless harping:

> How much longer are these wicked people going to complain against me? . . . Now [Moses] give them this answer, "You will die and your corpses will be scattered across this wilderness. Because you have complained against me, none of you over twenty years of age will enter that land. I promised to let you live there, but not one of you will. . . . You will die here in this wilderness. Your children will wander in the wilderness for forty years, suffering for your unfaithfulness, until the last one of you dies. . . . You will know what it means to have me against you. . . . I, the Lord, have spoken." (Lev. 14:27–35)

Consequently, the tribes wandered aimlessly in the desert. The Bible provides no time estimate for an express migration across Sinai from Egypt to Canaan. A fair approximation is perhaps one year. With divine punishment, the trek was lengthened to forty years. Imagine the agony of circling a wasteland for nearly two generations, an ordained death march if you were of the complaining slave generation, a lost youth if you were Sinai-born. Finally, the tribes reached the eastern border of Canaan, the Promised Land. The Lord wanted to make certain that the Israelites understood obedience was a matter of life or death:

> *Any one who sins deliberately . . . are guilty of treating the Lord with contempt, and they shall be put to death. (Num. 15:30–31)*

Still it was not yet time to pass into the Promised Land. First, there was unfinished business. God wanted revenge on a neighboring tribe that had led the Israelites astray, so he ordered Moses to punish the Midianites. Moses did not flinch. The death order would be carried out. He was God's servant, so Moses ordered his warriors to battle, and the result was fearsome:

> *They attacked Midian, as the Lord had commanded . . . and killed all the men. . . . The people of Israel captured the Midianite women and children, took their cattle and their flocks, plundered all their wealth, and burned all their cities and camps. (Num. 31:7–11)*

Having recently received the Ten Commandments—thou shalt not kill, steal, or covet among them—the divine order of retribution laid waste to those principles as surely as it did to the Midianites. For despite the death of all the men and plunder of all else, the carnage was not yet over. God's orders had not been followed strictly enough. Worried over again risking the Lord's wrath, Moses angrily faced the conquering Israelite army upon its return from its destruction of Midian:

> *Moses became angry with the officers. . . . He asked them, "Why have you kept all the women alive? Remember it was the women who . . . led the [Israelite] to be unfaithful to the Lord. . . . So now kill every boy and kill every woman who has*

had sexual intercourse, but keep alive for yourselves all the girls and all the women who are virgins." (Num. 31:14–18)

The plunder from the Midianites must be divided, and God commands Moses:

Divide what has been taken into two equal parts, one part for the soldiers and the other part for the rest of the community. From the part that belongs to the soldiers, withhold as a tax for the Lord one out of every five hundred prisoners, and the same proportion of the cattle, donkeys, sheep, and goats. (Num. 31:25–28)

The audit of the plunder meticulously proceeded. The Lord openly coveted his share of the war booty, including thirty-two virgins:

The following is a list of what was captured by the soldiers: 675,000 sheep and goats, 72,000 cattle . . . and 32,000 virgins. The half share of the soldiers was 337,500 sheep and goats, of which 675 were the tax for the Lord . . . and sixteen thousand virgins for the soldiers, of which thirty-two were the tax for the Lord. (Num. 31:32–40)

Why, we wonder, does the Lord want us to know such things? Thirty-two thousand girls distributed because they were virgins. How did the soldiers even know a girl's status? Certainly, these young girls witnessed unspeakable cruelty and destruction. God claimed thirty-two of them for himself. Scripture says nothing further of life's journey for the thirty-two thousand Midianite virgins.

Despite victory and the spoils of war, unhappiness prevailed. The people began to complain that nothing would grow. There was no grain, no figs, no grapes, and too little water. Such shortages are not surprising since the Bible's focus never strays from an arid patch between Egypt and Iraq, an area few farmers would consider a natural land of milk and honey. The tribes were unhappy and restless, and as they are wont to do under such conditions, the men began to have intercourse with the local Moabite women. Worse, the Israelites prayed to the local god. The Lord's wrath awaited them. The grisly death count was twenty-four thousand Israelites:

> *These women invited them to sacrificial feasts where the god of Moab was worshipped. The Israelites ate the food and worshipped the god Baal of Peor. So the Lord was angry with them and said to Moses, "Take all the leaders of Israel and, in obedience to me, execute them in broad daylight." Moses said to the officials, "Each of you is to kill every man in your tribe who has become a worshipper of Baal of Peor." (Num. 25:2–5)*

Twenty-four thousand died. God then ordered a second census. It was done and confirmed that the wandering death march had finally achieved its intended result of killing off anyone with a memory of Egypt:

> *There was not even one man left among those whom Moses and Aaron had listed in the first census in the Sinai Desert. The Lord had said that all of them would die in the wilderness, and except for Caleb . . . and Joshua . . . they all died. (Num. 26:64–65)*

Moses had displayed remarkable leadership and loyalty from the miraculous days in Egypt through the long years of harsh desert life in Sinai. Thus, his sadness must have been unbearable when he heard from God that he too was to be punished. For Moses, the sentence was worse than death. The biblical patriarch would never step foot into Canaan because he had suffered moments of doubt during decades of wandering. Who would not? Said God,

> *"Because you did not have enough faith to acknowledge my holy power before the people of Israel, you will not lead them into the land that I promised to give them." (Num. 20:12)*

The best prophet was not good enough. At the age of 120, a forlorn Moses pleaded his case for the chance to join his people in the Promised Land. The old prophet's pain is sweet poetry:

> *There is no god in heaven or on earth who can do the mighty*
> *things that you have done! Let me cross the Jordan River, Lord,*
> *and see the fertile land on the other side, the beautiful hill*
> *country and the Lebanon mountains. (Deut. 3:24–25)*

The God Moses served so well for forty years as a faithful instrument
for mayhem, miracles, and murders responded without mercy:

> *That's enough! Don't mention this again! Go to the peak of*
> *Mount Pisgah and look to the north and to the south, to the*
> *east and to the west. Look carefully at what you see, because*
> *you will never go across the Jordan. (Deut. 3:26–27)*

Moses never did cross the Jordan: he died within sight of the
Promised Land.

The Midianite slaughter was already part of a tradition. There
were no civil rights, and there were no civil warriors. Death was
cheap, quick, and often ordained by God as it had been earlier
with the Lord's instruction to avenge assaults against the Israelites
by the Amalekite tribe. This tribe had attacked God's people during their trek across the Sinai. The order for genocide was clear:

> *[B]e sure to kill all the Amalekites, so that no one will*
> *remember them any longer. Do not forget! (Deut. 25:19)*

So it came to pass. The deed was done.

The common perception is that the biblical Promised Land
was a vacant territory of fertile real estate ceremoniously gifted
by God to his people. In fact, it was long settled by many tribes
who believed it to be theirs. To them, the Israelites were outside
marauders stealing their homelands. They were correct, but God
had decided otherwise.

After Moses's death in Moab, Joshua was appointed leader.
It was finally time to begin the war to receive the gift. God gave
the order to attack:

> *All of this is the land, which I, the Lord, promised to give*
> *to your ancestors, Abraham, Isaac, and Jacob, and to their*
> *descendants. Go and occupy it. (Deut. 1:8)*

The Lord was in full battle gear. First, to allow for an invasion across the Jordan during its flood stage, God stopped the river from flowing:

> *As soon as the priests stepped into the river, the water stopped flowing and piled up, far upstream . . . and the people were able to cross over near Jericho. (Josh. 3:15–16)*

The first battle of the taking of the Promised Land was fought at Jericho. God provided Joshua a detailed battle plan for maximum devastation. It set the manner of action, the division of the war booty, and the assurance of vast death. Regarding the last two provisions:

> *Everything made of silver, gold, bronze, or iron is set apart for the Lord. It is to be put in the Lord's treasury. (Josh. 6:19)*

> *With their swords [the Israelites] killed everyone in the city, men and women, young and old. They also killed the cattle, sheep, and donkeys. (Josh. 6:21)*

The next battles occurred at Ai. The Israelites lost the first one but were successful in the second.

> *Then they went back to Ai and killed everyone there. (Josh. 8:24)*

The wars continued with a vast death toll, and the battles raged decade after decade. God was the general:

> *While the Amorites were running down the pass from the Israelite army, the Lord made large hailstones fall down on them. . . . More were killed by the hailstones than by the Israelites. (Josh. 10:11)*

When the Israelites required additional time during a battle to finish off their enemy, the Lord provided the necessary extra daylight:

> *The sun stood still and the moon did not move until the nation had conquered its enemies. . . . The sun stood still in*

the middle of the sky and did not go down for a whole day.
(Josh. 10:13)

Of course, God could have assured victory in the Wars of the Gift by performing a miracle far less incredible than stopping the sun in the sky. God had created a large earth; why not remove the pagans to France? Or convert them into true believers? Why not avoid war?

Despite decades of ruthless slaughter, the outcome of the Wars of the Gift was still in doubt when Joshua lay on his deathbed at the age of 110:

> *Joshua was now very old. The Lord said to him, "You are very old, but there is still much land to be taken; all the territory of Philistia and Geshur, as well as all the territory of the Avvim to the south. . . . There is still all the Canaanite country and Mearah . . . as far as Aphek . . . the land of the Gelbelites; all of Lebanon to the east. (Josh. 13:1–5)*

Although the Israelites' mortal leader was seemingly exhausted to the point of death, their Lord was urging the need for further conquest. The "gift" was not yet acquired. However, the divine cheerleading was unsuccessful, for after so many years of fighting and death, the Israelites lost faith in their God and turned elsewhere:

> *Then the people of Israel sinned against the Lord. . . . They stopped worshipping the Lord . . . and they began to worship other gods, the gods of the peoples around them . . . and served the Baals and the Astartes. (Judg. 2:11–13)*

People change gods with caution, especially under an announced penalty of death, and particularly when a tribal culture has for centuries lived under the reign of one god. The trauma of constant, brutal conflict and the loss of so many loved ones must have overwhelmed the people. The flood of tears must have become a river, carrying the people to a new religious home, one shared with the neighbors against whom they had warred. It was just as

God had prophesied, just as he had earlier told Moses. If the wars had been won, however, the victors would not abandon the God of victory. Soldiers and citizens do not change generals when the enemy raises the white flag.

Thus, the stone and wooden idols of Canaan must have offered at least the hope of hope, but the Lord offered only more decades of despair.

Predictably angry, a violent backlash by a spurned God was the result. The breadth and brutality of its scope is painful to read:

> *And so the Lord became furious with Israel and let raiders attack and rob them. He let the enemies all around over-power them. . . . Every time they would go into battle, the Lord was against them, just as he said he would be. (Judg. 2:14–5)*

> *[T]he Lord let them be conquered by Jabin, a Canaanite king . . . and he ruled the people of Israel with cruelty and violence for twenty years. (Judg. 4:1–3)*

Crushed and weeping, the Israelites prayed for help and received it from a relenting Lord. Then they sinned again, and then again, returning to their idols each time. So the Lord

> *let the Philistines rule them for forty years (Judg. 3:1).*

The tragedy of more than two centuries of cruel and deadly tribal warfare is incalculable. Impatient moderns fail to grasp the historic reach of military campaigns lasting more than two hundred years. It would be, for example, as if the American revolutionary war begun in 1775 at Bunker Hill were still continuing today.

How unimaginable are conflicts continuing for centuries, yet the wars of the Promised Land spilled blood for that long. In the end, the end was unclear.

Chapter Seven

I n addition to warring for Canaan, the Israelites engaged in brutal conflict among themselves. The brutish madness began with the gang rape of a concubine.

A Levite member of one of the twelve Hebrew tribes had taken a Bethlehem woman as his concubine, but she was unhappy with the man and returned to her father. The Levite followed her there, and after five pleasant days, they reconciled. Then they began the long journey home. At nightfall, they reached the Israelite town of Gibeah in the territory of the Benjamin tribe. By chance, an old man offered the weary travelers shelter for the night in his home. They were enjoying themselves there:

> *When all of a sudden some sexual perverts from the town . . .*
> *started beating on the door . . . "Bring out that man that came*
> *home with you! We want to have sex with him!" But the old*
> *man went outside and said to them, "Please! Don't do such an*
> *evil immoral thing! This man is my guest. Look, here is his*
> *concubine and my own virgin daughter. . . . Do whatever you*
> *want with them. . . . But the men would not listen to him. So the*
> *Levite took his concubine and put her outside with them. They*
> *raped her and abused her all night long and didn't stop until*
> *morning. At dawn the woman came and fell down at the door of*
> *the old man's house . . . Her husband got up that morning and*
> *when he opened the door to go on his way, he found his concu-*
> *bine lying in front of the house with her hands reaching for the*
> *door. He said, "Get up. Let's go." But there was no answer. So*
> *he put her body across the donkey and started on his way home.*
> *When he arrived, he went in the house and got a knife. He took*
> *his concubine's body, cut it into twelve pieces, and sent one piece*
> *to each of the twelve tribes of Israel. (Judg. 19:22–29)*

The tribal leaders were outraged at the sexual horror perpetrated by the men of Gibeah and demanded the guilty men be turned over to them. The Benjamin tribe refused. Four hundred and twenty-six thousand soldiers then prepared for battle. God gave battle instructions to the Israelites, but in the first conflict, they lost twenty-six thousand men. Again God gave instructions, but in the second battle, the Israelites lost eighteen thousand men, and they mourned bitterly, wanting to quit. But God told them:

> Fight. Tomorrow I will give you victory over them. (Judg. 20:28)

On the third day of battle, the Israelites killed 25,100 Benjaminites, thus, defeating the opposing army. Then, as we have seen time after time in the hideously bloodthirsty nature of biblical warfare,

> the Israelites turned back against the rest of the Benjaminites and killed them all—men, women, and children, and animals as well. They burned every town in the area. (Judg. 20:48)

The tragedy gets even worse. After the dust of tribal genocide had settled, some Benjaminite men still lived, but they no longer had wives, as all the women had been killed. The victorious Israelites became concerned that one of the ancient twelve tribes might die out, but they were adamant in refusing to provide women from their eleven tribes to the surviving Benjaminite men. Where to get the women? The Bible records the decision and the Lord's order:

> Go and kill everyone in Jabesh, including women and children. Kill all the males, and also every woman who is not a virgin. They found four hundred young virgins among the people in Jabesh. (Judg. 21:10–14)

They gave the four hundred virgins to the few surviving Benjaminites. Irony has no better home than the Bible.

Chapter Eight

In the important matter of government, the Lord was sovereign and his priests were the theocratic bureaucracy. However, this system did not work. The people were ungovernable in a mad epoch, and many felt a strong king was needed to quell the near anarchy. With understated eloquence, the Bible describes the era of some three thousand years ago:

> There was no king in Israel at that time. Everyone did whatever they pleased. (Judg. 21:25)

God heard the call for a king and advised against it. The divine analysis is concise and worthy material for a political science course, despite its ancient context:

> This is how your king will treat you. . . . He will make soldiers of your sons; some of them will serve in his war chariots, others in his cavalry. . . . Your sons will have to plow his fields, harvest his crops, and make his weapons. . . . Your daughters will be forced to make perfumes for him and work as his cooks and his bakers. He will take your best fields, vineyards, and olive groves, and give them to his officials. . . . And you yourselves will become his slaves . . . but the Lord will not listen to your complaints. (1 Sam. 8:11–18)

Such insightful observations regarding royal abuse would have softened the course of history if only the people had listened, but you could predict the result:

> The people paid no attention. . . . "No! We want a king, so that we will be like other nations." The Lord answered [by instructing Samuel], "Do what they want and give them a king." (1 Sam. 8:19–22)

Saul was appointed the first king of Israel, followed by David, then Solomon. The wars against other tribes continued and eventually reached their bloody conclusion. For a brief time under David, the Israelite kingdom was prosperous and included much of the Promised Land. King David was a favorite of the Lord, but like all men, imperfect. During his reign, he had an adulterous affair with the beautiful Bathsheba and then arranged to have her husband killed in battle. God was furious at the royal sin and intent on serious punishment. However, the divine sentence meted out to David— really, to *others*—reflects the still bizarre and vengeful ways of the Lord, which to moderns seems senseless and cruel:

> *Now, in every generation some of your [David's] descendants will die a violent death. . . . I [will] take your wives from you and give them to another man; and he will have intercourse with them in broad daylight. You sinned in secret but I will make this happen in broad daylight for all Israel to see . . . [and] your child will die. . . . A week later the child died.* (2 Sam. 1:10–14, 18)

King David had sinned, yet his wives—presumably innocent— are to suffer by being forcibly made the object of public displays of intercourse with strangers. Forced sex is raw violence in any society, but it is especially brutal when committed in the market square of a fundamentally religious society. By contrast, King David would still have many concubines to enjoy. More painful than the suffering wives is the moral drawn from the child's death. God chose to have David's innocent child die for the sins of his father. Future generations of innocents would also die violently.

The powerful and handsome king retained his throne and kingdom, but his sin doomed innocent women, a baby, and unspecified "descendants" because this was God's way during a time we do not understand.

Our search for an understanding of the biblical God takes us to another story from the epoch of David. The Lord commanded King David to conduct a census. David obeyed, and nine months later the results showed there were 1,300,000 men of military age. However, for unexplained reasons, the act of taking a census began to prey upon David's conscience. Remorseful, David said to God:

> *I have committed a terrible sin in doing this [census]! Please forgive me, I have acted foolishly. (2 Sam. 24:10)*

To the reader, it appears David did only as God commanded, yet the Lord was sufficiently angry to offer David a choice among three different punishments for his wrongdoing:

> *Three years of famine in your land or three months of running away from your enemies or three days of an epidemic in your land? (2 Sam. 24:12)*

David was reluctant to make the choice. Instead, he requested God to choose, because:

> *He is merciful. So the Lord sent an epidemic on Israel, which lasted from that morning until the time that He had chosen. From one end of the country to the other seventy thousand Israelites died. (2 Sam. 24:14–15)*

The Lord's execution by epidemic of seventy thousand innocents was the punishment for David's census error. King David's glory is legendary, but his offense was a death sentence for thousands.

The Israelites' third monarch was Solomon. Popularly believed to be a man of immense wisdom, King Solomon's reign gives important lessons in bad governance and the decline and demise that follow. Although Solomon was a wise young leader, his life is a clear example of the ruler who delights in the corruption that accompanies unchecked power. He married princess after princess either to consolidate or increase his rule. There were seven hundred such princesses, many of them foreign. Solomon brazenly violated God's law against intermarriage:

> *The Lord had commanded the Israelites not to intermarry with these people, because they would cause the Israelites to give their loyalty to other gods. (1 Kings 11:2)*

This prohibition against intermarriage is a common theme in the Old Testament and reflects one of many ways God displays a remarkable sense of insecurity. Over and over, he warns that foreign wives will convert their Israelite husbands to paganism. By contrast, the Lord never mentions foreign women converting to his worship.

Solomon opts for the faith of his foreign wives. It is rarely observed today that the "wisest man of all" chose pagan gods. Solomon abandoned the Lord of his youth for the many gods of his countless women:

> *He worshipped Astarte, the goddess of Sidon, and Molech, the disgusting god of Ammon. . . . On the mountain east of Jerusalem he built a place to worship Chemosh, the disgusting god of Moab. (1 Kings 11:5, 7)*

For the biblical crime—capital crime—of breaking the first commandment against worshipping any other god, a pained and vengeful Lord turns neighboring kings against Solomon and decrees that his kingdom will be lost *in the future* during the reign of Solomon's son and successor. Countless others will then die. However, Solomon seems unfazed by the announced capital punishments that are to begin *after* his death. Few leaders would be.

The most important lesson from the Solomon reign is the imperative of kingly excess, direct from God's political science course. Solomon filled his life with vast quantities of gold, ivory, a thousand wives and concubines, and forty thousand horses. With such trappings of majesty came high taxes and the very unwise forced labor of his people: ten thousand men were sent each month to toil in Lebanon, while seventy thousand porters and eighty thousand stone quarriers were rounded up for backbreaking construction work. The people complained bitterly against their heavy yoke. It seems Solomon was not as wise as myth suggests.

Nor was he as happy as having one thousand wives and concubines would suggest, at least to normal male fantasy. Was he happy? No, depressed:

A human being is no better off than an animal, because life has no meaning for either. They are both going to the same place—the dust. They both came from it; they will both go back to it. (Eccles. 3:19)

Soon after Solomon's death, the restive kingdom split in two; the northern half was known as Israel, and the southern half as Judah (hence the name "Jews"). Then, northern Israel abandoned the Lord and established temples for their new god, once again a golden bull calf.

"And so the people sinned" (1 Kings 12:30).

It is a wonder that the children of the exodus returned to the bull calf that caused them such massive grief in Sinai. Was the motivating psychological dynamic Solomon's observation that despair was everywhere?

Building stone temples to a bull-calf in violation of a fiercely vengeful God's first commandment suggests that wild desperation was in play and that the fight to control tribal faith must have been fierce.

The Bible records that the reigns of Hebrew kings led to despair. Wise Solomon had worshipped wooden statues, the Promised Land was never realized, and now the Hebrew kingdom was divided in two: Israel and Judea. Surely, a story of immense human interest and intrigue lies in the priestly decisions of that ancient tribal era. The robed holies in wind-blown tents—strange scents wafting through the reverberating air of heated discussions—voted to abandon the Lord of the heavens for a hand-crafted representation of a bull calf. We shall never pierce the darkness surrounding such a religious conversion.

We can only wonder at the degree of suffering to be endured before a God of miracles and commandments is bid farewell for the silent promises of burnished metal.

These were the people; these were the times from whence the Bible was delivered.

Chapter Nine

The two Old Testament books of Kings contain abstracts of the lives of the nineteen kings of Israel and the seventeen kings and one queen of Judah. The two Hebrew states warred almost continually with each other. Only about half the rulers in the Jewish kingdoms died a natural death. Sometimes entire royal families were consumed in murderous intrigues involving enemies or successors. The carnage is breathtaking.

Envision, for example, a momentarily serene queen Jezebel and then her gruesome death. She

> *[P]ut on eye shadow, arranged her hair, and stood looking down at the street from a window in the palace. As [King] Jehu [of Israel] came through the gate, she called out, ... "You assassin! Why are you here?" Jehu said to them, "Throw her down!" They threw her down, and her blood spattered on the wall and on the horses. Jehu drove his horses and chariot over her body, entered the palace, and had a meal... But the men who went out to bury her found nothing except her skull and the bones of her hands and feet. (2 Kings 9:30–35).*

The mayhem in 1 and 2 Kings is nearly boundless. In the account of the reign of King Menahem, who had earlier murdered King Shallum of Israel, we are told:

> *as Menahem was on his way from Tirzah, he completely destroyed the city of Tappuah, its inhabitants, and the surrounding territory, because the city did not surrender to him. He even ripped open the bellies of all the pregnant women. (2 Kings 15:16)*

Why did the Lord permit such horrors? His chosen people were choosing slaughter while God sent messages through prophets whom the people were unable to distinguish from profiteers. Surely, ordinary citizens tried to exist in ordinary ways free from the powerful, the corrupt, and the catastrophic, but God's history of the kings of the broken pieces of the Promised Land, from Solomon to the Babylonian invasions, leaves a believer shuddering.

Mosaic law, God's first constitution, was not working. The 613 laws were intended to control the worst aspects of individual behavior. Massive evil—five hundred thousand dead in only one of an infinite number of battles—was the instrument of kings, emperors, and imagined gods who obeyed no law. In reality, if good was to have a fighting chance against evil, then laws were needed to restrain the unrestrained. There were no elections, just knife against knife. No one then could imagine the restraints much later contained in the inspired writings of Thomas Jefferson or James Madison.

Chapter Ten

B eing a prophet in biblical times was a popular calling. This is not surprising in an age without newspapers, television, cinema, radio, magazines, or the Internet. In the absence of media, there was the message. Thus, many prophets roamed the countryside and towns of the Near East, spreading God's news, reciting poetry, and entertaining crowds.

Among the many, there were only a few prophets whom God established as genuine, and who held a holy franchise. They preached to the Israelites with the Lord's license to communicate his messages. Among the most famous was Isaiah—actually a series of "Isaiahs"—who lived in Jerusalem in the eighth, seventh, and sixth centuries BC. The language of God revealed through men writing as Isaiah is indeed powerful, but it is also extremely unsettling. Isaiah covers a time period of about 250 years following the split of the Israelite kingdom into northern Israel and southern Judah, together occupying approximately the territory of the present-day nation of Israel.

To feel the power of the Lord's message through Isaiah, imagine the great Sir John Gielgud playing the prophet on the London stage. Old and withered, with long, unsettled white hair, Sir John is Isaiah communicating God's torturous pain and demanding the good conduct of his people, conduct lost in the swirl of pungent odors from meaningless sacrificial ceremonies. Hear this well:

> *Earth and sky, listen to what I am saying! The children I have brought up have rebelled against me. Cattle know who owns them, and donkeys know where their master feeds them. But that is more than my people Israel know. . . . You are doomed, you sinful nation, you corrupt and evil people! . . .*

> *Israel, your head is already covered with wounds, and your*
> *heart and mind are sick. . . . I have had more than enough of*
> *the sheep you burn as sacrifices and of the fat of your fine ani-*
> *mals. I am tired of the blood of bulls and sheep and goats. . . .*
> *Stop all this evil that I see you doing. . . . See that justice is*
> *done—help those who are oppressed, give orphans their rights,*
> *and defend widows. (Isa. 1:2–17)*

God is furious, and he wants justice. He demands it, yet his keen interest in the vulnerable lasts but a moment. For in the next angry breath, the Lord decrees *death even to the widows and orphans:*

> *In a single day the Lord will punish Israel's leaders and its*
> *people; he will cut them off, head and tail. The old and hon-*
> *orable men are the head—and the tail is the prophets whose*
> *teachings are lies! . . . And so the Lord will not let any of the*
> *young men escape, and he will not show pity on any of the*
> *widows and orphans, because all the people are godless and*
> *wicked and everything they say is evil. (Isa. 8:14–17)*

In the pain of his disappointment and disgust, God seems to have lost his balance. The people are sinful for not doing justice to the widows and orphans; they are godless, wicked, and to be pun-ished. However, God does the same, breathlessly decreeing no divine pity for the orphans and babies. Why torture them?

Then God turns his wrath upon the women of Jerusalem, the holy city of God's temple, where displays of feminine allure will be turned into feminine baldness:

> *Look how proud the women of Jerusalem are! They walk*
> *along with their noses in the air. They are always flirting. They*
> *take dainty little steps, and the bracelets on their ankles jingle.*
> *But I will punish them—I will shave their heads and leave*
> *them bald. . . . Instead of using perfumes, they will stink; . . .*
> *instead of having beautiful hair they will be bald; instead of*
> *fine clothes, they will be dressed in rags; their beauty will be*
> *turned to shame. (Isa. 3:16–17, 24)*

God is tortured that his people act badly in so many ways. He is a father watching his children fall to dissipation, crudeness, and sacrilege. He will not forgive them. Instead he will doom them:

> *You are doomed! You buy more houses and fields to add to those you already have. . . . You are doomed! You get up early in the morning to start drinking, and you spend long evenings getting drunk. . . . You are doomed! You are unable to break free from your sins. You say, "Let the Lord hurry up and do what he says he will, so that we can see it. . . . You are doomed! You call evil good and call good evil. You turn darkness into light and light into darkness. . . . You are doomed! Heroes of the wine bottle! Brave and fearless when it comes to mixing drinks! But for just a bribe you let the guilty go free, and you keep the innocent from getting justice. (Isa. 5:8–23)*

This unrelenting anger finds its sword in God's call to Assyria and the Philistines—Israel's enemies—to "devour Israel." They are the instruments of divine punishment. These nations answered God's call to destruction, and Israel is devoured by foreign soldiers that

> *roar like lions that have killed an animal. (Isa. 5:29).*

The Lord uses pagan Assyria to wield his punishing club:

> *I use Assyria like a club to punish those with whom I am angry. I sent Assyria to attack a godless nation, people who have made me angry. I sent them to loot and steal and trample the people like dirt in the streets. (Isa. 10:5–6)*

The Lord's anger is consuming him. He keeps his word that he will torture his people on the rack of heartless and brutal war until in madness they eat their own children:

> *Everywhere in the country people snatch and eat any bit of food they can find, but their hunger is never satisfied. They even eat their own children! (Isa. 9:20)*

The prophet Jeremiah lived during the late seventh and early sixth centuries BC. Israel, the northern half of the formerly united Hebrew nation, was already under a heavy Assyrian hand. Now the Babylonians were threatening Judah, the southern half. Jeremiah, as a vehicle for God's voice on earth, was a sensitive man who agonized over the impending doom: Jerusalem was to fall, Judah was to be trampled, and the Jews sent into exile in Babylonia. However, as with Israel, the Lord's anger is uncontrollable. God summons Israel's enemies to destroy the nation of Judah, while he decrees horror:

> And so I, the Lord, will state my case against my people again. . . . No other nation has ever changed its gods, even though they were not real. . . . But my people have exchanged me. . . . And so I command the sky to shake with horror. (Jer. 2:9, 11–12)

> [Israel,] you are like a wild camel in heat, running around loose rushing into the desert. When she is in heat, who can control her? No male that wants her has to trouble himself; she is always available in mating season. (Jer. 2:23–24)

The fearsome Babylonian warriors crushed Judah. Babylonia thus became the Lord's pagan sword that sliced through Judah's heart, while a jealous and tormented God mocks his fickle people as they fall and die or are captured and exiled:

> Where are the gods that you made for yourselves? When you are in trouble let them save you—if they can! Judah, you have as many gods as you have cities. . . . I punished you, but it did no good . . . my people have forgotten me for more days than can be counted . . . But, Israel, you have had many lovers, and now you want to return to me! . . . Is there any place where you have not acted like a prostitute? You waited for lovers along the roadside, as an Arab waits for victims in the desert. (Jer. 2:28–29, 32; 3:1–2)

Why were the Israelites constantly turning away from their God? Whether their prayers were for real mercy or for real estate, they must not have been answered. Life remained cruel. Mass evil seemed to be everywhere. Make no mistake: modern-day sensitivities were not in play 2,500 years ago. The tribal God was one of boiling anger and rage. A new holocaust is coming:

> *People of Jerusalem, you are under siege! Gather up your belongings. The Lord is going to throw you out of the land; he is going to crush you until not one of you is left. The Lord has spoken (Jer. 10:17–18) . . . I will kill them in war and by starvation and disease. (Jer. 14:12) . . . Their bodies will be thrown out into the streets of Jerusalem, and there will be no one to bury them. This will happen to all of them—including their wives, their sons, and their daughters. (Jer. 14:16) . . . I will bring war, starvation, and disease on them until there is not one of them left in the land that I gave to them and their ancestors. (Jer. 24:10)*

Lest we forget, this is the Bible we revere and hold in sacred awe. It is God's own story, God's own justice. He has passed judgment and called in the executioners to destroy his children. Those not slaughtered in battle or dead through starvation were to be shipped off to a merciless, distant exile.

So, it came to pass that the Jewish kingdoms were destroyed. The death was horrific, and the survivors were marched off to slavery in Babylonia.

Years later, however, the Lord decided that his chosen had been punished enough, and he wanted them back in Jerusalem:

> *The Lord says, "The time is coming when I will be the God of all the tribes of Israel, and they will be my people. . . . People of Israel, I have always loved you, so I continue to show you my constant love. . . . Once again you will take up your tambourines and dance joyfully. (Jer. 31:1, 3)*

This time God did not want to be disappointed by a people who would love him and leave him. Therefore, he developed a new and vastly better plan of remaking mankind's heart so that it was good:

> *I will make a new covenant with the people of Israel and with the people of Judah. . . . The new covenant . . . will be this: I will put my law within them and write it on their hearts. I will be their God, and they will be my people. None of them will have to teach a neighbor to know the Lord, because all will know me. (Jer. 31:31, 33–34)*

Here then is the answer to God's prayers: program love directly into the hearts of his people, and they will never again abandon him. As he had once hardened Pharaoh's heart in Egypt, God would soften his chosen's hearts. The law was to be written on the heart, and the love of God it empowers would be strong because it would be natural.

Thus, the prophet Jeremiah had delivered the message to end all messages: human perfection. However, it was not to be and never happened. God did not replace evil with love in the hearts of mankind. Though possessing the divinely awesome power to rewire humanity for good, the Lord abandons his promise of perfection for that which always was: war—hundreds of years of war. First, he punishes Israel and disburses its people. Then he turns his divine wrath on Israel's neighbors because they took pleasure in observing the destruction.

Thus, the audience died for having enjoyed God's killing performance. The nation of Ammon was to disappear, as God declared:

> *You [Ammon] clapped your hands and jumped for joy. You despised the land of Israel. Because you did, I will hand you over to other nations who will rob you and plunder you. I will destroy you so completely that you will not be a nation anymore or be a country of your own. (Ezek. 25:6–7)*

Then God added Moab to the death list. Its tribes were to be destroyed because they believed Judah, the southern half of Israel, to be no better than any other nation:

> *Because Moab has said that Judah is like all the other nations I will . . . let the tribes of the eastern desert conquer Moab, together with Ammon, so that Moab will no longer be a nation. (Ezek. 25:8, 10)*

Continuing his revenge against those harming Judah, God promises genocide against Edom:

> *The people of Edom took cruel revenge on Judah. . . . Now I announce that I will punish Edom and kill every person and animal there. I will make it a wasteland. (Ezek. 25:12–13)*

There is more. God observes the Mediterranean commercial center of Tyre is cheering that "Jerusalem is shattered" (Ezek. 26:2). So, in the eleventh year of the Jewish exile, the Lord utterly destroys Tyre. The sin of its people appears to be only a businessman's glee over a rival's misfortune. Woe to such glee in the eyes of God:

> *I will put an end to all your songs, and I will silence the music of your harps. . . . I will make [Tyre] as desolate as ruined cities where no one lives. . . . I will send you down to the world of the dead. . . . As a result [Tyre] will never again be inhabited. (Ezek. 26:7–8, 13, 19–20)*

Words fail. And the void is filled by a Lord filled with anger:

> *All their evildoing began in Gilgal. It was there that I began to hate them [the Israelites] . . . I will not love them any more. . . . They will have no children, but even if they did, I would kill the children so dear to them. (Hosea 9:15–16)*

Kill the children? Why? Then this astonishing confession:

> *I was the one who brought famine to your cities, yet you did not come back to me. I kept it from raining when your crops*

*needed it most . . . still you did not come back to me. . . . The
locusts ate up all your gardens and vineyards. . . . Still you did
not come back to me. . . . I sent a plague on you . . . I killed
your young men in battle. . . . I filled your nostrils with the
stink of dead bodies. . . . Still you did not come back to me.
(Amos 4:6–10, 12)*

Words fail.

Chapter Eleven

(An Intermission)

We pause for a moment, among so many dead, to pay tribute to the beauty, wisdom, and morality that also find a home in the Old Testament. Surely, to honest readers, the Bible's bleakness is without equal, but so too is its beauty. Some may prefer the description "tragic beauty." The young God and his young subjects, a race of humans that was learning along with its Creator, display the entire universe of emotions.

Thus, there is great and remarkable beauty to be found throughout the Bible, even if it is not often the central focus of the text. For example, there are luminous love verses attributed to King Solomon, such as this excerpt from one of the most beautiful and erotic love poems of all ages, the Song of Songs:

> *Your lips cover me with kisses; your love is better than wine. . . . Take me with you, and we'll run away; be my king and take me to your room. We will be happy together, drink deep, and lose ourselves in love. No wonder all women love you! (Songs 1:2–4)*

> *How beautiful you are my love! . . . Your hair dances like a flock of goats. . . . Your teeth are as white as sheep. . . . Not one of them is missing . . . Your breasts are like Gazelles. . . . How beautiful you are my love; how perfect you are! (Songs 4:1–2, 5, 7)*

The Bible, particularly Proverbs, offers much famous advice that reflects moral and religious teachings. They are gems of eternal wisdom:

> *It is better to be an ordinary person working for a living than to play the part of someone great but go hungry. (Prov. 12:9)*

> *Why don't lazy people ever get out of the house? What are they afraid of? Lions? (Prov. 26:13)*

> *The reward for doing good is life, but sin leads only to more sin. (Prov. 10:16)*

The prophets of the Bible have much to say about righteous conduct:

> *When someone righteous stops doing good and starts doing evil, he will die for it. When someone evil quits sinning and does what is right and good, he has saved his life. (Ezek. 33:19)*

However, the poetry and proverbs that shoulder much of the Hebrew Bible's moral uplift are mere footnotes to the larger historical saga. Christians nevertheless find solace in them and seize on these bits of beauty and wisdom wafting among the boundless carnage. This human urge to grasp the strands of hope even amid divine holocaust also reflects an eternal truth. An honest reading of the Hebrew Bible stresses that sweet words of love and virtue are more than matched by stories of despair and bitterness, as in the Book of Job:

> *We are all born weak and helpless. All lead the same short, troubled life. We grow and wither as quickly as flowers; we disappear like shadows. (Job 14:1–2)*

Chapter Twelve

K ing Solomon, who famously had one thousand wives and concubines, untold riches, and wisdom, offers these God-inspired thoughts:

> *A human being is no better off than an animal, because life has no meaning for either. They are both going to the same place—the dust. They both came from it; they will both go back to it. (Eccles. 3:19)*

This is painful verse and anything but uplifting from an ancient tower of wisdom. However, Job and Ecclesiastes also survive as God's word. Certainly, within its more than eight hundred pages of fine print, the Old Testament has something for everybody, every passion, and every point of view. There seems to be proof for everything. Still, the main themes travel close to death and despair. Nevertheless, we will emerge from Old Testament trauma enlightened and, hopefully, ready to consider the possibility and promise of the eighteenth-century's final covenant.

In biblical times, the end was near almost all of the time. War, slavery, starvation, disease, grinding hardship, and religious oppression were the common lot. In any event, it is doubtful that many people lived many years. To make matters worse, however, there was an active apocalypse tradition in those ancient days. Later, Jesus also preached the coming end. Many before him, including Isaiah, preached the same message.

Through Isaiah, the Israelites learned of a forthcoming cataclysm, the destruction of the world:

> *The Lord is going to devastate the earth and leave it desolate. He will twist the earth's surface and scatter its people. Everyone will meet the same fate—the priests and the people,*

> *slaves and masters, buyers and sellers, lenders and borrowers,*
> *rich and poor. The earth will be shattered and ruined. The Lord*
> *has spoken and it will be done. . . . The people have defiled the*
> *earth by breaking God's laws and by violating the covenant he*
> *made to last forever. So God has pronounced a curse on the*
> *earth. (Isa. 24:1–2, 5)*

As a prophet, Isaiah was franchised by God to declare the coming cataclysm, but how could the people know if Isaiah spoke for God or was simply a raving madman? Did others also preach that God's lightning would shear the earth in half and torch the people? What clutter in the marketplace of ideas and idols; so many prophecies but so little truth. The Lord was angered by the many men masquerading as prophets. Soon enough, these impostors were courting death.

God announced death sentences for lying prophets, their listeners, and even the families of listeners:

> *The prophets are telling lies in my name; I did not send*
> *them, nor did I give them any orders or speak one word to*
> *them . . . their predictions are worthless. . . . I, the Lord, tell*
> *you what I am going to do to those prophets whom I did not*
> *send. . . . I will kill them in war and by starvation. The people*
> *to whom they have said these things will be killed in the same*
> *way . . . including their wives, their sons, and their daughters.*
> *(Jer. 14:14–16)*

The divine killing circle thus included the innocent families of those having merely heard the ungodly predictions. Of course, no one could be certain if the prophet on the corner was genuine or not. However, if a man on his way to the bazaar innocently stopped to listen to an "unlicensed" orator, a divinely determined death was to follow for the innocent listener and all his loved ones.

The proliferation of false messengers must have been truly overwhelming to provoke such a murderous response from God. Freedom of speech did not exist, nor was there freedom to listen or belong to a listener's family. If we can imagine a world without any of today's media—not a single electronic or printed word or voice—we may understand the strong vacuum pulling in so many voices who then gave out real or imagined news from the Lord and around the nation. News abhors a vacuum, and surely the gifted and the guileful could earn a shekel selling it.

Isaiah's prophetic words of total destruction were canonized as holy writ perhaps three hundred years after the apocalyptic event failed to occur. God wanted the message of doom to be delivered even if the doom wasn't. Why? While Isaiah and others bombarded the Jerusalem air with news of a shattering event, what were listeners to think? Were they to die tomorrow or next month? Would praying to the one God, or perhaps to a competing god, lead to a reversal of fortune? Was the final judgment really final?

In a contradiction of biblical proportion, Isaiah also gave us God's word that world peace and harmony were near. Many may recognize the prophet's sweet and poetic words describing a coming time when

> *wolves and sheep will live together in peace, and leopards will lie down with young goats. Calves and lion cubs will feed together, and little children will take care of them. Cows and bears will eat together, and their calves and cubs will lie down in peace. Lions will eat straw as cattle do. (Isa. 11:6–7)*

Unhappily this time, Isaiah got it wrong. What good news it must have been at the time; what wonderful conversation to share around the tribal campfires—if anyone believed it.

All news, then and now, is time sensitive. Listeners want to know what happened yesterday and what will happen tomorrow. What if 2,500 years ago Isaiah had shouted, "My friends, the news from our Lord is that in 2,500 years wolves and sheep will live together"? The crowd would have disappeared. The listeners wouldn't have listened, and one tribesman may have shouted back, "Isaiah, you toy with us. Is God without news for tomorrow?" That "lions will eat straw as cattle do" was another false— or still undelivered—prophecy from God through his prophet Isaiah. Such loving coexistence among biological enemies is a sweet thought, and the Almighty God surely has the power to make it happen, but 2,500 years later the word is stale and the message still wrong.

Meanwhile, in real time, Isaiah's female colleagues peddling news and magic were especially evil in God's view:

> *The Lord said, "Now, mortal man, look at the women among your people who make up predictions. Denounce them. . . . You women are doomed! You sew magic wristbands for everyone and make magic scarves for everyone to wear on their heads, so that they can have power over other people's lives. You want to possess the power of life and death over my people . . . in order to get a few handfuls of barley and a few pieces of bread. You kill people who don't deserve to die, and you keep people alive who don't deserve to live. So you tell lies to my people, and they believe you. . . . I am rescuing my people from your power, so that you will know that I am the Lord." (Ezek. 13:17–19, 23)*

The word does not provide a follow-up story; we do not know if such colorful ladies of message were doomed, or if their clients were rescued from them. What remains clear is that the best and the brightest of the prophets, such as Isaiah, were chosen by the Lord to communicate prophecies *that were monumentally wrong.*

We shall see below how another grossly mistaken prophecy from Isaiah—that of victory in yet another war then about to begin—was magically spun centuries later into the virgin birth of Jesus.

Isaiah left the biblical auditorium, but the performance was unchanged. To the southern half of Israel known as Judah, God had said in anger more than once, "My people, the day is coming." It finally did.

Under the violent armies of Nebucchadnezzar of Persia, Jerusalem became a boulevard of death, except for those survivors forced to march four hundred miles to exile in Persia. Through years and tears in that foreign land, the exiled Jews yearned for a return to the Promised Land.

Finally, God determined that his chosen had been punished enough. The exile was to end. By manipulating the Persian king's heart, the Lord prompted King Cyrus to issue the following command:

> *This is the command of Cyrus, Emperor of Persia. The Lord, the God of heaven, has made me ruler over the whole world and has given me the responsibility of building a temple for him in Jerusalem in Judah. . . . You [his people] are to go to Jerusalem and rebuild the Temple. . . . If any of his people in exile need help to return, their neighbors are to give them this help. (Ezra 1:1–4)*

Thus, the Jews finally returned to Judah from their exile in Persia, and the second Temple to God was built. Soon enough, however, the Jews shamed themselves once more in one of the endless opportunities to sin under scriptural law, this time by intermarrying:

> *Jewish men were marrying foreign women, and so God's holy people had become contaminated. The leaders and officials were the chief offenders. (Ezra 9:2)*

Intermarriage remained a threat to God. As always, he feared his people would abandon him in favor of wooden and metal idols worshipped by the foreign women. Seeing all this, God's servant and voice on earth, the prophet Ezra, tore in despair at his clothes, hair and beard. Crushed with grief he reviewed the tortured history of the Hebrews in a stunning lament:

> *O God, I am too ashamed to raise my head in your presence. Our sins . . . reach as high as the heavens. From the days of our ancestors. . . . Because of our sins we . . . have fallen into the hands of foreign kings, and we have been slaughtered, robbed, and carried away as prisoners. . . . We were slaves, but you did not leave us in slavery. You made the emperors of Persia favor us. . . . But now, O God . . . [w]e have again disobeyed the commands that you gave us . . . [you] told us that the land*

we were going to occupy was an impure land . . . filled . . .
from one end to the other with disgusting filthy actions. [Your
prophets] told us that we were never to intermarry with those
people . . . [W]e know that you, our God, has punished us less
than we deserve . . . how can we ignore your commandments
again and intermarry with these wicked people? (Ezra 9:6–7,
9–10, 12–14)

Ezra then felt God's command and began to carry it out. For three
months a committee

> *investigated all the cases of men with foreign wives. (Ezra*
> *10:17).*

A list of the sinners was prepared:

> *Masseiah, Eliezer, Jarib, and Gedaliah. They promised to*
> *divorce their wives, and they offered a ram as a sacrifice for*
> *their sins. (Ezra 10:18–19)*

Then, at the end of the very long list of names, there was the final
word in obedience to God:

> *All these men had foreign wives. They divorced them and*
> *sent them and their children away. (Ezra 10:44)*

Where did they go, these "sent away" women and children? Their
trail of tears must have watered the parched land unto the hori-
zon. Did they survive? We shall never know.

Certainly, the Jewish tragedy had to end some day, the priests
argued, because God would not permit it to last forever. Word that
such a day was coming was broadcast by the many prophets, both
real and imagined. Among them was Daniel, who probably lived
around the time of Alexander the Great. Israel had been under
Persian rule, and next came under Greek rule. Daniel delivered
the final scriptural word that the time of the *awful horror* was
coming. He spoke through one of God's angels:

> *The angel wearing linen clothes said . . . "[T]here will be a*
> *time of troubles, the worst since nations first came into exis-*

tence. When that time comes, all the people of your nation whose names are written in God's book will be saved. Many of those who have already died will live again: some will enjoy eternal life, and some will suffer eternal disgrace." [Daniel] asks, "But, sir how will it all end?" [The angel] answered . . . "Those who are wicked will not understand . . . only those who are wise will understand. . . . From the time the daily sacrifices are stopped, that is, from the time of The Awful Horror, 1290 days will pass." (Dan. 12:1–3, 8, 10–11)

Perhaps Daniel's groundbreaking news of an afterlife won him a chapter in the Hebrew Bible. Daniel, speaking for God, relayed the new message that worthy people may be resurrected while the wicked are destined for eternal damnation. Thus, hope could spring eternal into the beyond. With so much despair and no Prozac, a chance for a second chance was surely a welcome new leap of faith.

Some three centuries later, another Jewish rabbi quoted Daniel, preaching also that when the awful horror arrives, the righteous and the wicked would experience opposite destinies.

His name was Jesus.

PART TWO

THE NEW
TESTAMENT

Chapter Thirteen

The story of the troubled times in the Promised Land shows that misery generates its own form of creativity and guarantees an audience for those with answers. The end of the world was just such a message. Under the hard-luck circumstances of Judea, it would be a popular message that even God had had enough, that the world was so corrupt, cruel, and craven that a perfect Kingdom of God, by God, and for the believers in God, would arrive.

Into this milieu came baby Jesus in about the year 5 BC. Was there divine intervention in the birth of this future rabbi and savior? The Gospel according to Matthew tells the good news that Jesus is the promised savior, the one through whom God fulfills the ancient promises he made to his people in the Old Testament. As already seen, except for prophecies forecasting massive death, the divine promises were unfulfilled. However, just as some believers speak even today of the promised apocalypse as though issued last week rather than 2,500 years ago, the Jews of the Roman era quoted their ancient tribal prophecies with a contemporary passion.

Matthew's Gospel in the New Testament is an example of such Jewish reliance on the immediacy of seven-hundred-year-old prophecy carried along through the ages by oral tradition until set in parchment centuries later, however garbled it had become by politics and time.

Matthew begins Jesus' biography with his ancestry, which reflects the confusion surrounding his birth. This record of descent spans nearly two thousand years from the prehistory of the patriarch Abraham to Roman domination. There were neither hospitals nor birth records. It is doubtful that anyone even today could trace a family tree back through forty-two generations, or even half that, but all the individual names are provided:

> *This is the list of the ancestors of Jesus Christ, a descendant of David who was a descendent of Abraham. . . . So then, there were fourteen generations from Abraham to David, and fourteen from David to the exile in Babylon, and fourteen from then to the birth of the Messiah. (Matt. 1:1, 17)*

Thus, Matthew records and identifies by specific name twenty-eight generations from King David to Jesus. Meanwhile, the Gospel of Luke, which also names each ancestor in the line, declares the family tree consists of forty-three generations from David to Jesus, not twenty-eight. More remarkable is that *none* of those persons named in Matthew's line of twenty-eight from King David is named in Matthew's line of forty-three. Of further historic interest is that Luke takes the Jesus line back even earlier than King David, reaching through generations to Noah, ancient Methuselah, and ultimately to Adam "the son of God" (Luke 3:38). Only the Lord could know such things, but the gospelers disagree about what he knew.

Thus, Matthew and Luke cannot agree upon a single name in the family "step tree" of Jesus. *Step tree?* Yes. While completely disagreeing regarding the identity of Jesus' ancestors, both Gospels stress with pride the one-thousand-year blood trail from the revered King David to Joseph, but since Joseph was said to be Jesus' stepfather, the step-tree lineage is irrelevant: King David's blood did not run through Jesus' veins. Even if it did, it would be unrecognizable after one thousand years.

In contrast, the Bible provides no information regarding the Jewish girl Mary, Joseph's fiancée. There is nothing regarding her family background, physical fitness, intelligence, goodness, appearance, or most importantly, her psychological readiness to bear God's child. Did Jesus have his mother's eye color or his father's facial features? How was the complicated biology of reproduction accomplished without sperm impregnating an egg? Or was there sperm? If so, whose? Whose temperament did the child have? Whose intelligence? There are no answers; the Bible is silent.

Matthew wrote that God fathered the baby boy, although the important details are omitted:

> *This is how the birth of Jesus Christ took place. His mother Mary was engaged to Joseph, but before they were married, she found out that she was going to have a baby by the Holy Spirit. Joseph was a man who always did what was right, but he did not want to disgrace Mary publicly; so he made plans to break the engagement privately. While he was thinking about this, an angel of the Lord appeared to him in a dream and said, "Joseph, descendant of David, do not be afraid to take Mary to be your wife. For it is by the Holy Spirit that she has conceived. She will have a son, and you will name him Jesus—because he will save his people from their sins." (Matt. 1:18–21)*

Matthew tells us that the miraculous and immaculate conception of Jesus occurred to fulfill a prophecy made by Isaiah seven hundred and fifty years earlier:

> *Now all of this [virgin birth to Mary] happened in order to make come true what the Lord had said through the prophet [Isaiah], "A virgin will become pregnant and have a son, and he will be called Immanuel" (which means, "God is with us"). (Matt. 1:22–23)*

However, Matthew is mistaken; Isaiah made no such prophecy. Isaiah's brief verse said nothing about a virgin or a messiah. The virgin-birth story of divine intervention was elaborately spun from an unrelated single thread of the Book of Isaiah. Wrongly spun.

Moreover, the "virgin" story, so critical to Christian theology, appears only in Matthew among the four biographical gospels of Jesus. Why would three of four biographers omit arguably the most important basis of Christianity? The answer is clear when the prophecy is examined: Matthew, an unknown and unidentified ancient figure, was a very poor student of the Old Testament. By contrast, he was very creative in contorting Jewish prophecies to form a connection to early Christian writings.

Back to Isaiah. Recall that the Israelite kingdom had divided into a northern part called Israel and a southern half, Judah; together, they roughly constitute present-day Israel. In about the year 735 BC, the kings of Israel and Syria entered into an alliance to war against Judah. Alarmed, Judah's King Ahaz sought Isaiah's counsel. In response, the prophet Isaiah gave the message from God that Ahaz would prevail in the forthcoming war against his two enemies. According to Isaiah, the victory over Israel and Syria will occur this way:

> *[A] young woman who is pregnant will have a son and will name him "Immanuel." By the time he is old enough to make his own decisions, people will be drinking milk and eating honey. Even before that time comes, the lands of those two kings who terrify you will be deserted. (Isa. 7:14–16)*

Matthew's Gospel asserts this verse foretold the birth of Jesus. However, in 735 BC, Isaiah was declaring that within roughly eight to twelve years, a reasonable time for a biblical boy to begin making his own decisions, the attacking kingdoms of the Israeli-Syrian alliance would be defeated by Ahaz. It had nothing to do with a messianic prophecy.

Interestingly, the Old Testament's Book of Isaiah never discloses the outcome of the famous "victory in war" prophecy. Did Ahaz win? No, he was demolished. However, one must search elsewhere in the Bible, to the book of Chronicles, for the war news. Not only is Isaiah's message wrong regarding Ahaz's forthcoming military victory, but the Lord himself intervened to mastermind his horrific defeat. The contradiction is breathtaking:

> *Because King Ahaz sinned, the lord his God let the king of Syria defeat him. . . . The lord also let the king of Israel defeat Ahaz and kill 120,000 of the bravest Judean soldiers in one*

> *day. . . . Even though the Judeans were their own relatives,*
> *the Israelite army captured 200,000 women and children as*
> *prisoners. (2 Chron. 28:5–6, 8)*

Ahaz's defeat was a slaughter. One hundred and twenty thousand of his Judean soldiers fell and became rotting corpses in the desert sun. Added to this was the horror of two hundred thousand widows and orphans captured, an ugly fate in a world where brutality is undiminished even among relatives.

We cannot know why God had Isaiah give King Ahaz such incredibly wrong counsel. Perhaps it was a divine retribution; Ahaz had earlier sacrificed two of his own sons to a pagan idol.

And what of a prophet who gets it wrong? The Lord is clear:

> *You may wonder when you can tell when a prophet's message does not come from the Lord. If a prophet speaks in the name of the Lord and what he says does not come true, then it is not the Lord's message. (Deut. 18:20)*

Matthew's second error was to omit the twelve-year time frame—the duration of a boy's childhood—within which Isaiah prophesied his king's victory. Christ was born more than seven hundred years after Isaiah assured Ahaz that success would soon arrive

Matthew's third error was originating the Christian idea that Isaiah prophesied a virgin birth. However, it is now accepted by many, perhaps most, scholars that Isaiah actually used the term "young woman." The American Bible Society, a mainstream Christian organization that translated directly from the old Hebrew, is careful to note the "virgin" error as a translation issue:

> *The Hebrew word here translated "young woman" is not the specific term for "virgin," but refers to any young woman of marriageable age. The use of "virgin" in [Matthew] 1:23 reflects a Greek translation of the Old Testament, made some 500 years after Isaiah. (see footnote k, p. 617; see also Reader's Digest Bible, 1982, at page 372, "Behold, a young woman shall conceive")*

Today, the two-thousand-year-old translation blunder is almost universally acknowledged by objective scholars. However, at the time of Matthew, scripture from eight hundred years earlier was being read in Greek rather than Isaiah's Hebrew. Matthew was clearly creative: he borrowed the *virgin* who had been mistranslated from *young woman*, discarded the time-limited military purpose, and then declared Jesus the virgin-born baby messiah who fulfilled Isaiah's prophecy—which never referred to a messiah to begin with. For Matthew, the boy from Isaiah's story of victory in war was recast into the Prince of Peace. While the transformation is fascinating, the evidence for "divine" is absent. Such is the winding path of prophecy across eight hundred years, from Hebrew oral tradition to Christian gospel.

Further questions arise about the Mary and Joseph parenting of God's only son. Of course, the very notion of a deity having a child is extraordinary, although pagan precedents such as Zeus' fathering of Hercules are numerous. In any event, the Lord's parenting options would have been endless. For example, God could have floated his child to earth on a cloud, landed him in the lap of Augustus Caesar in Rome, and made the mightiest man on earth bow down to the divine baby. The world would have been in boundless awe. Or God could have delivered his son as a fully-grown man, just as Adam was, riding into Jerusalem on a winged white stallion and declaring freedom from the Romans for the Israelites. The word of God's greatness would then have been well documented and known throughout the world.

All this *could* have happened. Miracles such as these or innumerable others were available to the Lord of the universe. Any such public birthing of a new God-son would have overcome all questions about the boy's divine heritage. Moreover, an open and welcoming presentation would have quickly gained worldwide acceptance for the Lord and his new covenant. All mankind would have heard the story of the divine birth, and the newly faithful would have been innumerable.

Instead, God chose to act in secret and even ran afoul of his own immutable law. The virgin mother Mary was an unknown Jewish teenager already promised in marriage. She was engaged to Joseph. God's eternal law said that sex with another man's fiancée was a sin punishable by death:

> Suppose a man is caught in a town having intercourse with a young woman who is engaged to someone else. You are to take them outside the town and stone them to death. . . . In this way you will get rid of this evil. (Deut. 22:23–24)

Thus, God is said to have broken his own unchanging law against evil in order to have an anonymous girl bear a son in secret. And, this impregnation assertedly was pursuant to a nonexistent virgin prophecy from seven hundred years earlier. It is fair to ask, was there divine intervention?

Additional perspective regarding the birthing of Jesus is found in Matthew's other efforts to use Jewish prophecy to prove events. In so doing, Matthew consistently misreads the ancient texts. Perhaps, and no one knows, the unknown Matthew had no access to biblical parchment for ready reference.

In any event, the references continue. Jesus was born in Bethlehem in Judea during the reign of King Herod. Matthew writes that men who studied the stars, sinful behavior under the Mosaic Code, came looking for a baby future king:

> Soon afterward, some men who studied the stars came from the East to Jerusalem and asked, "Where is the baby born to be the king of the Jews? We saw his star when it came up in the east, and we have come to worship him." (Matt. 2:1–2)

God's casting of a new star through the heavens to mark the birth of a king shows again an activist Lord at work displaying infinite power, star-making power. But the demonstration of omnipotence always raises the question of why God so often makes odd choices in the use or withholding of his divine strength. The unfathomable is again on display in Matthew's postnatal story of baby Jesus.

As the three visitors continued their search for the baby, they again saw the star:

> *[I]t went ahead of them until it stopped over the place where the child was. (Matt. 2:10)*

The earth's sun is a star. No one could locate a house by looking beneath it. The earth's moon, poetically speaking, might be considered a star, but no one could locate a residence by looking beneath it. Whatever star tracked Jesus' birth location would be a remarkable miracle since its nearness to earth—sufficient to identify the place of the child's birth—would create an immense disaster. Imagine the spectacle of a burning star in the sky so near a village that travelers could use it for a road sign to a dwelling. Thousands, at the least, would have rushed out to view the star or panic wildly in the streets. Either way, chaos would follow. Surely, historians would have recorded the event if it occurred, though only the Bible reports it.

King Herod of Judea, having heard news of the birth of a future king, decided to kill the baby. That being so, God had the option of simply changing Herod's heart as he had changed the hearts of Pharaoh, King Cyrus of Persia, and numerous others in the Bible. Merely the tiniest miracle, a well-placed dream of peace during Herod's sleep, would have worked to restrain the king's death squads. However, instead of pacifying Herod's heart through the tranquilizing effect of a nighttime fantasy, the Lord used a dream to instruct stepfather Joseph to flee for his life. Thus, awakened

> *Joseph got up, took the child [Jesus] and his mother, and left during the night for Egypt, where he stayed until Herod died. This was done to make come true what the Lord had said through the prophet, "I called my Son out of Egypt."*
> *(Matt. 2:14–15)*

Matthew was wrong again. There was no such prophecy to be fulfilled. Had God merely forgotten what his own prophet had said? Was Matthew groping in the dark, having no library available for Bible reference, or was the gospeler shaping scripture to tell a tale?

We look to the source. The Hebrew prophet Hosea preached in the northern kingdom of Israel in the middle 700s BC. At the time, God was nearly crazed with jealousy because his people had again abandoned him for idols. So angry was the Lord over Israel's infidelity that he says through Hosea:

> *The people of Israel are like a plant whose roots have dried up and which bears no fruit. They will have no children but even if they did, I would kill the children so dear to them. (Hosea 9:16)*

After threatening death to the children, the Lord turns momentarily nostalgic, recalling the youthful Israel he had rescued from slavery in Egypt centuries before. In musing about the past, God uses the words "called him out of Egypt," which Matthew mistakenly calls a future prophecy, and wrongly attaches to baby Jesus. Rather, it is a metaphor for the young nation of Israel. God, speaking through the prophet Hosea, says:

> *When Israel was a child, I loved him and called him out of Egypt as my son. But the more I called to him, the more he turned away from me. My people sacrificed to Baal; they burned incense to idols. Yet I was the one who taught Israel to walk. . . . They refuse to return to me . . . and Assyria will rule them. . . . War . . . will destroy my people. (Hosea 11:1–3, 5–6)*

God kept his word. In 721 BC, Israel was destroyed by Assyria, God claims, for "sinning by making metal images to worship." However, none of this tragic history had anything to do with Matthew's claim that Joseph and his family fled by night to fulfill Hosea's words. Israel had been "called out of Egypt" some 1,300 years before Jesus was born, and the Lord, through Hosea, was waxing nostalgic for that long-waned era. Indeed, there had not even been a prophecy in Hosea's verse. Only a sigh. Nothing more. The Lord sighed for the past but gave no sign for the future.

Errors aside, one wonders why a loving God would choose to have his newborn flee by night only steps ahead of the king's sword in order "to make come true," a seven-hundred-year-old prophecy, *even if* there had been one. A new baby and a tired mother would be bundled on a donkey and trekked across the Sinai desert to pagan Egypt. The ancient Israelites had spent forty years climbing that trail. The dangers would be enormous. Moreover, doing so would mean breaking God's command to Jews against ever returning to Egypt (Deut. 17:16). Besides, who actually cared? Who cared whether a child was "coming out of Egypt"? Proving paternity of a God-son could be achieved in countless dramatic and observable ways besides having him come out of Egypt.

Of course, the wiser option would have been to kill King Herod. It would be a justifiable homicide, self-defense in the face of the king's attempted murder of the baby. Instead, the evil flowed unchecked in Herod's veins as he went on a killing quest to destroy the would-be king:

> *[H]e gave orders to kill all the boys in Bethlehem and its neighborhood who were two years old and younger . . .*
> *(Matt. 2:16)*

Consider the cruelty of Herod's order and the absence of divine intervention. Armed centurions broke down perhaps hundreds of doors to pull infants away from horrified parents. In the tug of war between soldiers and mothers, the infants' tender limbs are stretched like rope. The soldiers win. Screaming infants are then butchered by swords piercing their soft bellies. The parents are frozen in immeasurable agony, grieving for a better world with a more merciful God. Yes, baby Jesus escapes, but why did all the other babies have to die?

According to Matthew, the infant Jesus was carried off to be hidden in exile, surely a strange role for a young God. There, the family waited for King Herod's death. Why did God prefer the continuation of Herod's bloody kingship to his son's right to live in safety in his homeland? Herod was an evil king who would have killed Jesus in a wink if ever he laid his sword upon the child. Nonetheless, he kept his throne and Jesus kept his distance.

Years later the Lord sent an angel to Egypt to signal the coast was finally clear for Mary, Joseph, and Jesus to return:

> *After Herod died, an angel of the Lord appeared in a dream to Joseph in Egypt and said, "Get up, take the child and his mother, and go back to the land of Israel, because those who tried to kill the child are dead. So Joseph got up, took the child and his mother, and went back to Israel. (Matt. 2:19–21)*

However, mortal danger still lurked ahead. When Joseph heard that Herod's son had succeeded his father as king of Judea, he refused to go to Bethlehem despite the Lord's green light. Because God was then convinced the danger to the baby was real, he revised his earlier dream-instructions to Joseph. Pursuant to the amended dream, the family proceeded to Nazareth rather than Bethlehem. As a result of this happenstance rescheduling, Matthew asserts yet another ancient prophecy came true about the life of Jesus:

> *And so what the prophets had said came true: "He will be called a Nazarene." (Matt. 2:23)*

But the ancient Jewish prophets never said such a thing.

In following a checklist of nonexistent or erroneous ancient prophesies, God's interest in his "son" seems secondary to improving the track record of long-dead prophets. Jesus was exiled to a hostile foreign land when, as God's son, he would have had endless educational and social opportunities at home. Of what use was exile from the land of his future ministry? Indeed, the Bible records not a word about Jesus' years in the land of Pharaoh, presumably because there was nothing worth noting. The lost years in Egypt served only the impossible purpose of fulfilling—claims Matthew—a nonexistent prophecy.

This unfortunate detour wasted much of Jesus' short life. While the Gospels are conflicting, it appears that Jesus' ministry lasted only about eighteen months before his crucifixion. Since

Jesus' death came at about age thirty-four, why did God waste precious years of his son's life for absolutely nothing? In Jesus' day, there were respected historians and philosophers, as well as Jerusalem crowds, before whom the Lord could have openly published any miraculous news. Instead, the divine hand turned to puppetry, looping Jesus from asserted prophecy to asserted prophecy in secret. Was Matthew wrong? Was there no divine intervention in the life of Jesus, but only the gospeler's desire to make it seem so?

Chapter Fourteen

ollowing his return from Egypt, Jesus next notably appears in Matthew as a mature man who meets John the Baptist. John was a renowned rabbi who drew large crowds from the province of Judea and adjacent areas. He wore camelhair clothes and dined on locusts and honey. People came in droves to confess their sins to John and be baptized in the Jordan River. Jesus was among them. However, John's principal message was in the Jewish apocalyptic tradition of doom:

> *Turn away from your sins . . . because the kingdom of heaven is near. (Matt. 3:2)*

John the Baptist and Jesus were ministering soul mates. The message was that God's arrival to fix a broken world was near. Preaching the kingdom of heaven was the right message at the right time. People were spiritually ready for the long-predicted end of time when their painful lives would be renewed in joy. This prophecy stretched back nearly eight hundred years, and the fact that it enjoyed eternal appeal could only mean that the yearning of a desperate people was also eternal. The religious, superstitious, and social mix that welcomed the end-of-time message was indeed a miserable stew.

Part of the misery was the absence of any notion of modern liberty. Roman arbitrariness was the rule. When his friend John the Baptist was imprisoned, Jesus took this as a sign to leave. Did he feel his life was at risk? In any case, Jesus traveled to Galilee and there commenced his brief ministry and adopted John's apocalyptic chant:

> *From that time Jesus began to preach his message: "Turn away from your sins, because the kingdom of heaven is near!" (Matt. 4:17)*

His message was identical to John's. The kingdom of heaven was coming:

Jesus went all over Galilee, teaching in the synagogues, preaching the good news about the kingdom, and healing people who had all kinds of disease and sickness. . . . Large crowds followed him from Galilee . . . from Jerusalem, Judea, and the land on the other side of the Jordan. (Matt. 4:23, 25)

However, there was a problem: the arrival of the kingdom of heaven never happened. It was yet another chapter in the already ancient tradition of falsely broadcasting doom. Nevertheless, Jesus earnestly preached his message, demanding certain behavior in order to earn salvation from the coming time of horror. The end was near, Jesus said:

Happy are those who know they are spiritually poor; the Kingdom of Heaven belongs to them! (Matt. 5:3)

Happy are those who are persecuted because they do what God requires; the Kingdom of heaven belongs to them! (Matt. 5:10)

Jesus' teaching of "Happy are those who are persecuted" was out of touch with life in the Roman colony in which he lived. Persecution was joyless, as Jesus later came to know firsthand. When he began his ministry, he had an opportunity to suffer through the torment of John the Baptist. Rabbi John was Jesus' role model and considered by the people to be a prophet, the Lord's spokesman on earth. Jesus believed John the Baptist to be even greater than that:

[A] prophet? Yes indeed, but you saw much more than a prophet . . . I assure you that John the Baptist is greater than anyone who has ever lived. (Matt. 11:9, 11)

"Greater than anyone who had ever lived," said Rabbi Jesus of Rabbi John. As it turns out, John was arrested and jailed by King Herod for his sermons against marriage between a brother and

sister. John was being persecuted. While John remained imprisoned, King Herod held a birthday party for himself, during which
he was so pleased with his niece's dancing that he offered her the
gift of anything. She said:

> *Give me here and now the head of John the Baptist on a*
> *plate! (Matt. 14:8)*

> *Herod was committed to pleasing his young niece, so he had*
> *John beheaded in prison. The head was brought in on a plate*
> *and given to the girl. (Matt. 14:10–11)*

Was John happy to be persecuted? Did Jesus believe his decapitated friend was in a happier place? Jesus' own turn was coming
soon enough.

Jesus continued his ministry of apocalypse as part of his
broader teachings. The story is essentially a one-act play: the
world will end, and the righteous will enter the heavenly paradise that follows. However, God still appeared unwilling to break
his post-flood promise to Noah: "Never again will I put the earth
under a curse." Did Jesus really have divine authority to broadcast a repeal of the Lord's first covenant?

Nevertheless, Jesus was a believer, and his faith in the next
kingdom was absolute. So strongly did Jesus carry the prophetic
banner of doom that he told his listeners to love their enemies:

> *You have heard that it was said, "Love your friends, and*
> *hate your enemies." But now I tell you: love your enemies and*
> *pray for those who persecute you, so that you may become the*
> *children of your Father in heaven. (Matt. 5:43–45)*

Christ taught to love one's enemies and wish persecutors well.
This volume proposes instead the inspired teachings of America's revolutionaries, who believed that God intended them to free
themselves of persecution by getting rid of their enemy. Christ's
vision was of pacifism, while the Founding Fathers went to war.
We wonder which remedy reflects divine inspiration in the battle
against evil?

Jesus preached the message of loving one's enemies, but the love was only pre-apocalyptic. After the apocalypse, when the earth is cleaved and eternal placement assignments are handed out, Jesus said sinners would forever burn. In the coming kingdom the non-blessed will be sent away to a fiery hell until time itself disappears. Jesus had said, "Do not take revenge on someone who wrongs you." He also said, "Happy are those who are merciful to others." But the truth seems to be, do what is necessary to reach the kingdom, then watch the bad guys burn unmercifully as the Lord takes eternal revenge. Be nice now and divine revenge will come soon enough.

Those in the pulpit may disagree, but Christ had no love for the pulpit, teaching against its very existence. The grandiose churches and cathedrals of Christendom violate Christ's message that all prayer be private:

> When you pray, do not be like the hypocrites! They love to stand up and pray in the houses of worship and on the street corners, so that everyone will see them. . . . But when you pray, go to your room, close the door, and pray to your Father, who is unseen. And your Father, who sees what you do in private, will reward you. (Matt. 6:5–6)

Pray in private. Then your father, the Father of all mankind, will see and reward you. Christian leaders universally ignore this part of the message of Christ and call the faithful to communal prayer. Most people would agree that church attendance is beneficial. However church attendance was not the message of Christ. His warning against congregations, like many of his teachings, was intended as an aid for his generation's divine rescue from evil in the coming new age.

One of Jesus' most famous teachings is about revenge and self-protection. The message is undeniably sweet, but also it is undeniably inapt for a world not ending in the next few months:

> You have heard that it was said, "An eye for an eye, and a tooth for a tooth." But now I tell you: do not take revenge on

someone who wrongs you. If anyone slaps you on the right
cheek, let him slap your left cheek too. And if someone takes
you to court to sue you for your shirt, let him have your coat
as well. And if one of the occupation troops forces you to carry
his pack one mile, carry it two miles. When someone asks you
for something, give it to him; when someone wants to borrow
something, lend it to him. (Matt. 5:38–42)

We all have had a lifetime in which to ponder such advice. Does
experience teach us to give the left cheek after the right one has
been slapped? Do we live that way? Would we want our children to live that way? Most importantly, in today's rough world,
would we want our national government to act that way? Voluntarily carrying an enemy soldier's pack an unrequested extra
mile is treason, not reason. Jesus preached otherwise because he
believed in pre-apocalyptic love. It is worth recalling that during
World War II the pacifist Mahatma Gandhi suggested to the British that they lay down their firearms and welcome the Nazis with
open arms. We are thankful the British prayed to Jesus the pacifist
but wisely chose not to follow him.

Jesus preached for only eighteen months. His doomsday
message was able to survive such an abbreviated career. Always,
he counseled the need to be ready. Part of that preparation was to
leave your job, your family, and regular life behind and go with
Jesus. Answering such a call would rupture families, and Jesus
seems to have intended exactly that:

[D]o not think that I have come to bring peace to the world.
No, I did not come to bring peace, but a sword. I came to
set sons against their fathers, daughters against their mothers,
daughters-in-law against mothers-in-law; your worst enemies
will be the members of your own family. (Matt. 10:34–36)

Your own family will be your worst enemy—what a sad message.
Like his father, Jesus was ferociously jealous of divided loyalty.
He insisted on messianic dedication to his cause: leave everyone,
leave everything, and love only me:

Those who love their father or mother more than me are not fit to be my disciples; those who love their son or daughter more than me are not fit to be my disciples. Those who do not take up their cross and follow in my steps are not fit to be my disciples. Those who try to gain their own life will lose it; but those who lose their life for my sake will gain it. (Matt. 10:37–39)

The messianic element of the Jesus movement served to disrupt families by setting son against mother, and brother against brother. This discord even extended to his family. Matthew tells of Jesus' rejection of his mother even though the fifth commandment demands parental respect. Just as he counseled sons to leave their families for his mission, Jesus seems to have abandoned his own family:

Jesus was still talking to the people when his mother and brothers arrived. They stood outside asking to speak with him. So one of the people there said to him, "Look, your mother and brothers are standing outside, and they want to speak with you." Jesus answered, "Who is my mother? Who are my brothers? Then he pointed to his disciples and said, "Look! Here are my mother and my brothers! Whoever does what my Father in heaven wants is my brother, my sister, and my mother." (Matt. 12:46–50)

What a human moment. Mother Mary came to speak to her son who was in a business meeting with his colleagues. "I'm busy, Mom, this is my new family, and I'm talking with them now. Sorry." This is an old story with resonance for all the ages.

Some took up Jesus' call and attached themselves to his roving ministry. One follower, Peter, asked Jesus:

We have left everything and followed you. What will we have? (Matt. 19:27)

Jesus' answer reflects a strange messianic vision totally foreign to contemporary society. Most people would shudder at the notion of parents abandoning children and family in order to follow an itinerant rabbi. Yet, Jesus asked siblings and spouses to do exactly that for the promise of riches and eternal life:

> *You can be sure that when the Son of Man sits on his glorious throne in the New Age, then . . . everyone who has left houses or brothers or sisters or father or mother or children or fields for my sake, will receive a hundred times more and will be given eternal life. (Matt. 19:28–29)*

Eternal life promised by a uniquely charismatic figure. Family abandonment was part of the pre-apocalyptic message to join his group on the road to salvation. The threat of not doing so was terrifying as Jesus told of an unparalleled disaster in the offing, repeating Daniel's three-hundred-year-old broadcast of the awful horror

> *You will see the awful horror of which the prophet Daniel spoke . . . [T]he trouble at that time will be far more terrible than any there has ever been, from the beginning of the world to this very day. Nor will there ever be anything like it again. (Matt. 24:15, 21–22)*

The most terrible days in the history of earth will soon arrive. The sun, moon, and stars will be reprogrammed:

> *Soon after the trouble of those days, the sun will grow dark, the moon will no longer shine, the stars will fall from heaven. . . . Then the sign of the Son of Man will appear in the sky; and all the peoples of earth will weep as they see the Son of Man coming on the clouds of heaven with power and great glory. The great trumpet will sound and he will send out his angels to the four corners of the earth, and they will gather his chosen people from one end of the world to the other. (Matt. 24:29–31)*

When it is over, Jesus will ride out of heaven on clouds to the sound of a great trumpet. All the people will weep. The visions are out of this world. Were the tales of all these celestial wonders divinely inspired?

For eighteen months, Jesus trekked from Galilee to Jerusalem, walking a wave of apocalyptic fervor. There were no movies, TV, magazines, radio, or newspapers. There were rumors and rumor-mongers in the alleys and bazaars. Many gifted speakers held court on dusty corners to announce the news as they knew it. Whom to believe? What to believe? There was the Bible, of course, and those few able to read the parchments had the power of information in a world of ignorance and superstition. Those with the gift of voice could gather crowds eager to listen and be entertained, if not enlightened and saved.

When, Jesus, when will it happen? When will the earth shatter and the glorious day arrive?

No one knows . . . when that day and hour will come— neither the angels in heaven nor the Son; the Father alone knows. . . . Watch out, then, because you do not know what day your Lord will come. If the owner of a house knew the time when the thief would come, you can be sure that he would stay awake and not let the thief break into his house. So then, you also must always be ready, because the Son of Man will come at any hour when you are not expecting him. (Matt. 24:36, 42–44)

Be ready. Always be ready. It may happen at any time. But what? What will happen? Jesus dramatically preaches about an end in which he will be royally enthroned and then separate the blessed from the damned:

When the Son of Man comes as King and all the angels with him, he will sit on the royal throne, and the people of all nations will be gathered before him. Then he will divide them into two groups, just as a shepherd separates the sheep from the goats. . . . Then the King will say to the [righteous], "Come you that are blessed by my Father . . . and possess the kingdom which has been prepared for you." . . . Then he will

say to [the others], "Away from me, you are under God's curse!
Away to the eternal fire which has been prepared for the Devil
and his angels!" (Matt. 25:31–34; 41)

Is Jesus saying that he, rather than God, will be sitting on the
royal throne, dividing the good souls from bad? So it appears.
However, his words are blasphemy to the Israelites, fire from the
tongue of a man who would occupy God's throne and from there
identify evildoers. The Israelites believed only in the one God,
and no one else could do God's work. Jesus was courting trouble
because blasphemy was a capital offense under the law.

However, Jesus was a smart rabbi in a crowded occupation competing for listeners. And there were many. His delivery included parables, healings, demon exorcisms, revolutionary
dietary concepts, assertions of heavenly enthronement, and a
reputation for literally fighting off the devil. These were all ele-
ments of a revolutionary effort to reform Judaism. The audiences
warmed to miracles. Jesus was a realist who understood that con-
vincing people to believe would be aided by demonstrations of
magical power. Thus, he deputized his twelve assisting disciples
and gave them miraculous powers:

[G]o to the lost sheep of the people of Israel. Go and preach,
"The kingdom of heaven is near! Heal the sick, bring the dead
back to life, heal those who suffer from dreaded skin diseases,
and drive out demons." (Matt. 10:6–8)

Outside of the Bible, no record refers to any miracle by Jesus or
his disciples. The Roman world of the Near East included historians, philosophers, and teachers. Detailed records from the
period exist, but aside from a reference that a "Jesus" lived and
preached, there is no historical evidence of Jesus' life, miraculous
or mundane.

Chapter Fifteen

J esus was passionate about his ministry. He demanded loyalty and obedience. Failure in either respect brought horrific retribution. Jesus instructed his disciples that those who refused to aid his cause would suffer a fiery death:

> When you come to a town or village ... go into a house and say, "Peace be with you." If the people of that house welcome you, let your greeting of peace remain; but if they do not welcome you, then take back your greeting. And if some home or town will not welcome you ... I assure you that on the Judgment Day God will show more mercy to the people of Sodom and Gomorrah than to the people of that town! (Matt. 10:11–15)

Thus, the messengers of the gospel of the coming kingdom of heaven would either be received with a welcome or be rejected upon penalty of death. Jesus knew his revolutionary message would cause uproar, and he predicted an awful response:

> Watch out, for there will be those who will arrest you and take you to court, and they will whip you. . . . People will hand over their own brothers to be put to death, and fathers will do the same to their children; children will turn against their parents and have them put to death. Everyone will hate you because of me. . . . I assure you that you will not finish your work in all the towns of Israel before the Son of Man comes. (Matt.10:17, 21–23)

So much gruesome death was to accompany Jesus' message. Fathers will have their children killed. Children will have their parents killed, Jesus says, as the command to avoid sin is spread.

What a horrific specter his words raise. With such extraordinary power at his command, why must God bear witness to so much death in the delivery of his message of a better world? Why not gladden the hearts of the people? Why not make come true God's most important prophecy delivered through Isaiah:

> *[God] will settle disputes among great nations. They will hammer their swords into plows, and their spears into pruning knives. Nations will never again go to war, never prepare for battle again. (Isa. 2:4)*

If God can make that prophecy, why not make it come true? That is the mission of the Final Testament: when every nation on earth has a democratically elected government functioning within the outlines of the American revelation, Isaiah's reputation for pre-science will soar, but not before.

Two thousand years ago, however, the aggressive tribal cultures of the Near East and Roman imperialism were part of a historical mix without restraints upon violence. Even Jesus spoke of fomenting awful familial homicides. Fortunately, Jesus joined Isaiah as wrongly predicting an imminent apocalypse; whether the mass of family deaths he foresaw occurred is unknown.

Jesus carried his brief ministry across Israel until he neared Jerusalem, where he and his disciples stopped at the Mount of Olives. There, Jesus instructed two of his disciples:

> *Go to the village . . . and . . . find a donkey tied up with her colt beside her. Untie them and bring them to me. And if anyone says anything, tell him, "The master needs them," and then he will let them go at once. (Matt. 21:2–3)*

Jesus' instruction implied that if no one questions the taking of the animals, just steal them. "Thou shall not steal" was overlooked. Such animals had considerable value, so we ask why would Jesus steal? The answer lies in Matthew's failed efforts to show that ancient prophecies were coming true through Jesus. Thus, Matthew has Jesus explain the theft of the donkey and colt to his disciples as necessary:

> *In order to make come true what the prophet had said: "Tell the city of Zion, Look your King is coming to you! He is humble and rides on a donkey and on a colt, the foal of a donkey."* (Matt. 21:4–5)

However, Matthew was wrong again. Did Jesus' entrance into Jerusalem on a donkey fulfill the Hebrew prophet Zechariah's words more than five centuries earlier? Zechariah had been concerned with the restoration of Jerusalem following the exiling and return of its people. In joyous anticipation of a New Jerusalem *in his day* and with a reestablished monarchy, Zechariah was inspired by God with this prophecy:

> *Shout for joy, you people of Jerusalem! Look, your king is coming to you! He comes triumphant and victorious, but humble and riding on a donkey—on a colt, the foal of a donkey. (Zech. 9:9)*

Zechariah's highly dramatic prophecy was for a new Jewish king five centuries *before* Jesus, when a newly freed and leaderless people were adrift in a pagan world. His was a message of great hope in a war-torn place. Zechariah had the message his listeners must have craved: our new king is coming, humble but victorious! Imagine, however, if he had shouted with joy to his listeners, whose own lives may stretch to forty years, "Dear people of Jerusalem, five hundred and fifty years from today, our glorious new king will arrive and give us joyous salvation—praise our Lord!" What would the people think of news slated for more than ten lifetimes into the future? Zechariah's listeners would have stoned him for being a fool.

Matthew's gospel places Jesus on a stolen donkey to make Zechariah appear prescient. God could have placed Jesus on a golden chariot to make the Lord appear omnipotent. God didn't, so Bible readers are left with Matthew's story, which is erroneous. How can we be sure?

It is erroneous because Zechariah's donkey-borne king was prophesied in the next biblical verse to make peace among all nations and rule from sea to sea. He told his fellow Israelites:

> *Your king will make peace among the nations; he will rule from sea to sea, from the Euphrates River to the ends of the earth. (Zech. 9:10)*

The Euphrates is in Iraq; therefore, the victorious king of Zechariah's prophecy in 550 BC would soon arrive on a donkey, bring peace to all nations, and rule a territory from Iraq to the very ends of the earth. Yet another false prophecy. Zechariah was wrong, and so was Matthew. Still, however, the idea of peace among the nations continues to live. It always will. With the Final Testament, that hope may finally be realized.

The story continues. Jesus rode his stolen donkey triumphantly into Jerusalem. People spread their cloaks and olive branches on the road as the animal stepped along. The crowd grew and cheered:

> *The whole city was thrown into an uproar. "Who is he?" the people asked. "This is the prophet Jesus, from Nazareth in Galilee," the crowds answered. (Matt. 21:10–11)*

The people's prophet had arrived to celebrate Passover, the Jewish holiday commemorating the Lord's "passing over" the homes of the Hebrews in Egypt in the process of killing the Egyptian firstborn. Rabbi Jesus was perhaps thirty-four years old when he arrived in the religious center of Judaism; his Jewish ministry was less than two years old. Having traversed Roman-dominated Israel preaching the coming end of time, Jesus suggests that the long-awaited intervention was very near. He proceeded to God's home, the great temple, and preached:

> *Countries will fight each other; kingdoms will attack one another. There will be earthquakes everywhere, and there will be*

famines. These things are like the first pains of childbirth. . . .
"You will see 'The Awful Horror' standing in the place where
he should not be." Then those in Judea must run away to
the hills. . . . Pray to God that these things will not happen
in the winter! Nor will there ever be anything like it again.
(Mark 13:8–20)

With fanfare, Rabbi Jesus had arrived in Jerusalem to spread his
strong message. Was he happy with his mission?

Happy are those whose greatest desire is to do what God
requires. (Matt. 5:6)

Doing what God requires was in fact Jesus' calling. His life
seemed a model of happiness. However, that was not the case.
His soul was tortured; his burdens too many. He prayed, as the
sorrow in his

heart was so great that it almost crushes [him]. . . . "My
Father, if it is possible, take this cup of suffering from me!"
(Matt. 26:38–39)

The cup of suffering was not taken from Jesus; in fact, much
more was added to it. The crucifixion was coming.

Chapter Sixteen

J udaism's priests and elders made plans to have Jesus arrested and put to death. Such plotting seems in line with the endless power struggles of the Bible and the perpetual quest for more influence by those who have it or want it. Jesus was seen as being in the way; therefore, he was disposable. Moreover, his claim to a future throne in heaven from which he would separate good people from bad was a blasphemous usurpation of God's power—unless, of course, Jesus was God. Neither the Jewish priests nor the Roman administration thought so.

When Jesus entered Jerusalem, crowds welcomed him as a prophet. For nearly one thousand years, Jewish prophets captivated the attention of people hungry for news from their God. They were the broadcasters, the evening-news anchormen of their epoch. Nevertheless, the prophets were still mortals; special men chosen by the Lord to be his servants. Jesus was so welcomed. Throughout his ministry, Jesus' disciples watched their rabbi, listened to his teachings, and followed his commands.

It is strange, therefore, that one of them, Judas Iscariot, for thirty silver coins, later betrayed his rabbi by giving damning evidence to those plotting to have Jesus killed. Why strange? If you believed Jesus to be the only son of an omnipotent and vengeful God, and if you believed Jesus was imbued with divine power to walk on water and raise the dead, then you would not cross such a man-God. Or have him sent to the cross. Not for thirty silver coins, or even thirty million. Terror would hold you in check with a vision of instant and gruesome death. Reason tells us that Judas did not believe he betrayed Jesus the God, but Jesus the mortal rabbi.

The Roman soldiers arrested Jesus. The incident could have—should have—ended right there. The Lord could have

torn the Romans asunder before they laid a finger on his son. Or
Jesus could have defended himself. If he had earlier raised the
dead, surely he could have lowered the living, but that was not
the script. Matthew writes that it was Jesus' choice to be taken by the
Romans. He allowed it. He even welcomed it. He had armies of
angels at his disposal capable of slaying Roman legions. However, God's script for Jesus was that he die "to make come true
what the prophets wrote in the scriptures." But there were options.
God could have canceled the old prophecy, and declared a new
one. God could have commanded Jesus to live to be one hundred
with a ministry reaching to China. Jesus, if he were the Son of
God, could himself have ordered such a fate or better, spreading
the new word farther, faster, more completely, and far beyond the
Near East so that all may be saved, but it was not to be. Under
arrest, Jesus tells his captors that he submits and will face death
in order that the scriptures come true:

> *Don't you know that I could call on my Father for help, and
> at once he would send me more than twelve armies of angels?
> But in that case, how could the Scriptures come true which say
> that this is what must happen? . . . But all this has happened
> in order to make come true what the prophets wrote in the
> Scriptures. (Matt. 26:53–56)*

What must happen? Why must it happen? Right there, at that
moment, God and Jesus could and should have made better history. The scriptures need not come true. They rarely did. Prophecies almost always went unrealized. The Hebrew prophet Isaiah,
so relied upon by Matthew, prophesied many wondrous events
that time has yet to accommodate:

> *Lions will eat straw as cattle do. . . . There will be nothing
> harmful or evil. (Isa. 11:9)*

> *The deaf will be able to hear . . . the blind . . . will open
> their eyes. . . . It will be the end of those who will oppress oth-
> ers. (Isa. 29:18–21)*

> *The new Jerusalem I make will be full of joy . . . those who*
> *live to be a hundred will be considered young. (Isa. 65:17–24)*

Jesus said God had the power to send twelve armies of angels to rescue him and kill the plotters. Why not do it? Is the answer really "in order to make come true" one of Isaiah's ancient prophecies? If fruition waited six hundred years, why not one hundred more? What was the rush, in an ironic sense? Jesus had preached for less than two years. Did he have to die at age thirty-four?

All such probing is beside the point, for once again *Matthew's Gospel was mistaken. There was no prophecy calling for Jesus' martyrdom.*

The focus is again the book of Isaiah, a remarkable work of jumbled beauty and terror. It is a soulful cry, full of incoherent rage, disjointed poetry and gruesome accounts of war. Isaiah is wailing against evil and wailing for goodness. There is unbearable sadness over Israel's pain and loss, and unbearable destruction for its people. He is hope one moment and barbaric death the next. Navigating Rabbi Isaiah's writing is a journey of breathtaking confusion, bouncing along all the arteries of the human condition.

Who is Isaiah, the man upon whom Matthew relies so much and so incorrectly for his gospel of Jesus as God? No one knows, but his works cover a period of some two hundred and fifty ancient years, making it certain that several men were reporting God's word under the pen name "Isaiah." There is no record of their identities or even of their existence outside the Bible. God once said of his prophet:

> *My servant Isaiah has been going around naked and bare-*
> *foot for three years. This is a sign of what will happen to*
> *Egypt and Ethiopia. (Isa. 20:3)*

Could it be that in such a fundamentalist age, an important prophet would live life unclothed? It is scripture, but it is also strange. Nevertheless, for the gospeler Matthew, Isaiah was the Hebrew Testament source for prophecies of Jesus' virgin birth and martyred death. Thus, the religious impact of Isaiah through

Matthew has been enormous. Yet, as we earlier saw, the ancient Hebrew said nothing about the birth of Jesus, nor, as we shall see, did he foretell his death. It seems that *Matthew was wrong from Jesus' beginning to Jesus' end.*

The explanation for Jesus' martyrdom finds its source in Isaiah's story of the "suffering servant." Although it was the prophet's habit to prophesy in the future tense (i.e., something *will occur),* the servant story is placed in the *past.* About the servant, Isaiah wrote:

> *We despised him and rejected him; he endured suffering and pain. No one would even look at him—we ignored him as if he were nothing. . . . But because of our sins he was wounded, beaten because of the evil we did. We are healed by the punishment he suffered, made whole by the blows he received. (Isa. 53:5)*

Matthew says that Jesus voluntarily died at age thirty-four to fulfill these words. However, the verse is part of Isaiah's description of Jewish enslavement in Babylonia and God's decision to return his servant people to Jerusalem:

> *Israel, remember this: remember that you are my servant. I created you to be my servant, and I will never forget you. (Isa. 44:21)*

Isaiah often used "servant" as a metaphor for Israel and did so several times within the same Babylonia/Jerusalem history relied upon by Matthew. Could Jesus somehow have been the suffering servant? No. First, there is the unusual description of the servant as physically ugly:

> *Many people were shocked when they saw him; He was so disfigured that he hardly looked human. (Isa. 52:14)*

The Bible nowhere suggests that Jesus was disfigured beyond recognition as a human being. If Matthew is to be accepted, then Jesus has a new and distinctly unpleasant look. On the other hand, numerous metaphors throughout the Bible refer to Israel as God's servant, constantly suffering, a prostitute, ugly, and displaying various aspects of moral, physical, and metaphorical disfigurement.

Isaiah then continues with his story of the servant who had neither dignity nor beauty:

> *Who could have seen the Lord's hand in this? It was the will of the Lord that his servant grow like a plant taking root in dry ground. He had no dignity or beauty to make us take notice of him. There was nothing attractive about him, and nothing would draw us to him. (Isa. 53:1–2)*

This is not the Jesus of common understanding. Jesus without dignity or beauty? Unnoticed by the people because there was nothing attractive about him? This description does fit, however, as a metaphor for the Israel of Isaiah's history lesson. God found it ugly and undignified that his chosen had turned to idols. By contrast, Jesus surely displayed dignity and was greatly noticed. He was thronged by people throughout his ministry and then cheered as a prophet as he rode his donkey into Jerusalem.

Finally, and importantly, is the absence of a *prophecy* in Isaiah's story of the suffering servant. It was a tale told in the *past* tense. By contrast, Isaiah's many prophecies use the future tense. Thus:

> *Nations will never again go to war, never again prepare for battle. (Isa. 2:4)*

> *The Lord is going to devastate the earth and leave it desolate. He will twist the earth's surface and scatter its people. (Isa. 24:1)*

Who was the past-tense suffering servant? Almost certainly, it was the metaphorical story of a disfigured Israel shuttled off to Babylonia. There, God's servant suffered, was beaten, and eventually made whole when the Lord decided to return his "servant" to Jerusalem.

Whoever was Isaiah's subject, this disfigured and unnoticed servant suffered long before Jesus was born. Jesus' death had nothing to do with the gospel's explanation. There was no prophecy foretelling Jesus' death, and his voluntarily choosing death to satisfy the nonexistent is a biblical tragedy turned historic tragedy beyond words.

The final episode in the life of Jesus continues. He was taken before a council of the priests. "Tell us if you are the Messiah, the Son of God," they order. At that moment, God and Jesus had yet another chance to right history. Jesus could have said, "Yes, I am. And to prove it, I hereby make a wreath of red roses appear upon your priestly head." If it actually happened that on that bald priestly pate there suddenly appeared a beautiful garland of twelve perfect roses, then history would have unfolded very differently. However, for want of a dozen roses or a well-pitched bolt of lightning or an army of angels, the Father gave up his son. Instead of performing miracles to win release, Jesus inflamed the priests by saying:

> *I tell all of you: from this time on you will see the Son of Man sitting at the right side of the Almighty and coming on the clouds of heaven! (Matt. 26:64)*

If ever it were true that actions speak louder than words, the moment for action had arrived. Instead, Jesus used only words in response to the prosecuting priests, and blasphemous words at that, for no man sits at God's side and travels on clouds. There is only one Lord. Blasphemy was punishable by death under God's law, and Jesus' persecutors were emboldened when mere words rather than miracles were offered in defense.

An army of angels called into action by Jesus would have meant freedom. God could have done whatever he pleased. Parting a sea, stopping the sun, saving a son—this is the work of a God doing things right. It didn't happen, so we wonder, was God really the Father?

Jesus was next taken before the Roman governor, Pontius Pilate:

> *"Are you the king of the Jews?" Pilate asked. "So you say,"
> answered Jesus. (Matt. 27:11)*

Jesus would say no more. He was asked about the priestly accusations against him, but he said no more. Later, jealous Jewish authorities and the crowds called for Jesus' death. The Roman governor Pilate gave them what they wanted: an order for Jesus' crucifixion. The prisoner was then whipped, but Jesus said no more. Nor did he call for the armies of angels, or otherwise reach for the freedom he claimed was within his grasp, causing us to wonder, was God the father?

In the custody of Pilate's soldiers, Jesus was taunted, spat at, hit, and mocked with the shout "Long live the King of the Jews!" He was then crucified on a wooden cross. The soldiers threw dice to draw for Jesus' clothes. Above his head was the sign "This is Jesus, the King of the Jews." Skeptical onlookers shouted for Jesus to free himself so they may believe in him:

> *People passing by shook their heads and hurled insults at Jesus: "You were going to tear down the temple and build it back up in three days! Save yourself if you are God's Son! Come on down from the cross! . . . If he will come down off the cross now, we will believe in him! He trusts in God and claims to be God's Son. Well, then, let us see if God wants to save him now!" (Matt. 27:39–40, 42–43)*

The people stared up at the crucified Rabbi Jesus. They said among themselves, "If he will come down off the cross now, we will believe in him!" Of course, he didn't come down. That was not to be. Who could look at Jesus on the cross and believe his father, if he were the God of the Bible, would watch the torment and stand aside? Even the faithful had growing doubts as death grew near. Doubt became disappointment, then anger, and then mocking torment.

Who would expect them to believe? Who would expect God's son to be so abandoned by God?

Sitting in our reading chairs trying to imagine this scene brings us up far short. Take a moment and look at the palm of your left hand. Focus on it. Try and imagine a six-inch-long iron spike, roughly hewn, cracking through your flesh, your sinews, and your bones as a stone mallet drives it into wood now stitched hard against the back of your hand. Blood pours from the wound. The pain shoots through the body as the brain reports a monstrous agony. The right hand is then nailed. Unbearable pain. More blood. The weight of the hanging body fiercely pulls down, ripping the flesh. More nails smash through one foot, then the other, burning you into the wood, squirting more blood and flesh. Dizziness. Bowels yielding their all. Sagging body weight pushes down against the iron holding fast flesh that aches to drop. Whatever the world used to be, it has become blank. It is all raw flesh, mangled muscle, and bone. And rock-parched thirst. A cough then causes ceaseless twitching and more bolts of flashing pain. It is all too unreal to believe so there is no more reality.

God was a witness to the death of Jesus. The Lord abandoned the man on the cross, and his word describes the end as it came:

At noon the whole country was covered with darkness, which lasted for three hours. At about three o'clock Jesus cried out with a loud shout . . . "My God, my God, why did you abandon me?" . . . Jesus again gave a loud cry and breathed his last. (Matt. 27:45–46, 50)

Wielding miraculous power, divine power, the Gospel God made the sun disappear so that his son went out in darkness. With miraculous paternal detachment, God made his love disappear so that his son went out in loneliness. How utterly bewildered Jesus must have felt. How urgent those feelings must have been to break through the immeasurable pain and find expression in a last utterance before death: "My God, my God, why did you abandon me?"

When the Roman soldiers came to take down the dead Jesus, was God orchestrating the fulfillment of yet another old prophecy? To be gruesomely fulfilled on his son's torn body? Thus, one of the soldiers (and God surely had the power and motive to stop this):

> *plunged his spear into Jesus's side, and at once blood*
> *and water poured out. This was done to make the scripture*
> *come true: "Not one of his bones will be broken." And there*
> *is another scripture that says, "People will look at him whom*
> *they pierced." (John 19:34, 36–37)*

If you had all the power in the universe to do good, if you were omnipotent beyond all imagining, would you let your son die this way?

So it was that Rabbi Jesus died on the Roman torture stake virtually alone. Although he had chosen martyrdom, his last breath ached with the pain of abandonment. There is no contemporary record of his death. However, all his contemporaries complicit in his death—Judas, the disciples denying allegiance to Jesus, the prosecuting priests, the crowd demanding his blood, and the serious Roman governor responsible for local order—must have believed the accused was not the son of a vengeful god in heaven.

No man would knowingly sentence an authentic god to death because a real god cannot die, and a vengeful one kills in ways too horrible to imagine. It would be the case that in Jerusalem's back rooms and government offices, relevant participants carefully weighed the facts and risks before opting for Jesus' death. If they were wrong, then their own lives and fortunes were there for the taking by a god quick to seek revenge. Rabbi Jesus was hardly cause enough for the smart men of Jerusalem's elite to risk their all.

Political men are calculating men, and those trawling the muddy waters of Jesus' undoing surely believed the troublesome rabbi was a mortal man born to mortals. Jesus himself never said otherwise. However, had there been any Son of God rumors, the local power brokers clearly rejected them.

The horror of the crucifixion suggests that God did as well.

Chapter Seventeen

The Bible tells Jesus' story four times in the Gospels of Matthew, Luke, Mark, and John. Of course, all versions are equally considered scripture, the inspired word of God. This volume emphasizes Matthew's biography of Jesus in order to present a single coherent version. Still, the gospels when taken together cover only a small part of Jesus' approximately thirty-four years: his birth, a few days when he was twelve, and his last eighteen months or so. God's inspiration to his son's biographers was inexplicably limited as to time. Consequently, thirty-two of Jesus' thirty-four years—more than 90 percent of his life—remain blank in the father's story of his asserted son's life.

The Gospels were written years after Jesus died and were not formally canonized as godly scripture until the fourth century AD. What editing may have occurred during those centuries is unknown. Equally unknown is the effect of translations upon content or purpose, as Jesus' story and words went from ancient Aramaic across decades of oral tradition into ancient Greek, then Latin, and much later into English. Religious and political agendas also have their ways with words and undoubtedly influenced the Bible's present form.

In addition, the four Gospels are often at sharp variance with each other. For example, as earlier noted, Matthew identifies twenty-eight descendants in the line from King David to stepfather Joseph, while Luke names forty-three, with the further bizarre quirk that not a single name appears on both lists. God may have inspired both Gospels, but the inspirations are wildly different. However, it is not the purpose of this volume to identify the many story conflicts from one Gospel to the next. Numerous scholars have already trod that ground. Still, it is fair to point out that the New Testament begins with a birth story hanging from vastly different family trees and ends with a rising-from-death story hanging upon seventy-two hours of four-way confusion.

The resurrection story begins with the placement of Christ's body following its removal from the torture stake. Matthew's Gospel asserts that it was put in a well-guarded sepulcher with a secure rock sealing its entry. The other gospels omit the details. According to Matthew, when the sun began to rise, Mother Mary and Mary Magdalene went to see the sepulcher. Next, Matthew describes an earthquake followed by an angel rolling back the stone from the entrance. The other books say nothing about an earthquake or a door-opening angel. Matthew says the angel outside informed the two Marys that Jesus had been raised and to go and see the place where he had been lying. The angel then told them to go and tell the disciples, whereupon they quickly left. They hurried to tell the disciples when suddenly Jesus himself appears to them, and they take hold of his feet and worship him. Matthew then relates that the eleven disciples were informed to go immediately to a mountain in Galilee. They did. Jesus was there on the mountain, and they worshipped him.

John's gospel says it was dark at the sepulcher, and that Mary Magdalene went alone. She saw the stone had been taken away and went to tell the disciples. Peter and the other disciples went to the tomb, saw it was empty, and went back home. Mary arrives a second time, and John says that she saw two angels, both seated. John writes that it was Jesus Christ himself who told Mary Magdalene the news that he would be going back to his Father. John's version has the eleven disciples meeting secretly in a locked room with Jesus appearing to them on two different occasions.

Luke says it was Mary Magdalene, Joanna, and some other women who arrived and found the stone rolled away. He says there were two angels, both standing. Luke then relates that Jesus met with two of his followers walking on the road to Emmaus, seven miles from Jerusalem. He stays and eats with them, but when breaking bread, reveals himself to them and disappears from their sight. Luke then places the meeting with the eleven in a house in Jerusalem, far from Galilee, but at the same time.

Mark writes that the angel was already seated inside the sepulcher. He also writes that the women, seeing the opening to the sepulcher, went inside, where they were told of Christ's having risen. Finally, Mark writes that after the resurrection, Jesus appeared in another form to two of the disciples as they walked in the country, and that these two then told the other nine, who didn't believe them. He then tells of Jesus appearing to the eleven disciples while they were eating.

In all the versions, the post-Resurrection meetings were very private affairs, away from the public or any public authority able to record the miraculous event. If Christ's intent was to convince the world that he had risen, his actual conduct shows an attempt to keep it secret. The conflicting and confusing details in the four versions underscore the success of this stealth. Does this seem like the work of the Lord? If he wished to win the faith of the people, why not a rousing public resurrection accompanied by the same angels and trumpets Jesus said would accompany his public return to earth?

Then the sign of the Son of Man will appear in the sky; and all the peoples of earth will weep as they see the Son of Man coming on the clouds of heaven with power and great glory. The great trumpet will sound and he will send out his angels to the four corners of the earth. (Matt. 24:30–31)

Experience suggests that people acting in secret have something to hide. By comparison, as we shall later see, when America's founders worked to resurrect their tortured colonies, they assembled in a public building in Philadelphia for all the world to see. Were not both events equally worthy of public view? Then why was Jesus' resurrection a jumbled secret, while liberty's was put on universal display?

The other half of the post-crucifixion story, the ascension to heaven, is also critical to the "divine intervention" inquiry. Several times Jesus foretold of his rising to take his place at God's side. At his trial before the priests, Jesus refused to defend himself and instead told his accusers that they will see "the Son of Man sitting at the right side of the Almighty and coming on the clouds of heaven."

So what do the four Gospels say about this essential point? Matthew does not say a word. Despite including many insignificant details in his lengthy telling of the Jesus story, Matthew omits any mention of a heavenly rising. Instead, Matthew ends his gospel with an enthusiastic farewell meeting between Jesus and his disciples, set on a Galilean hill:

> *I have been given all authority in heaven and on earth. Go,*
> *then, to all my peoples everywhere and make them my dis-*
> *ciples. . . . And I will be with you always, to the end of the*
> *age. (Matt. 28:18–20)*

The Gospel according to John also lacks any mention of an ascension. However, it places the final meeting at Lake Tiberius rather than on a Galilean hillside. There, Jesus met with his disciples, where they ate fish and broke bread. John then concludes with a mysterious flourish that leaves us guessing:

> *Now, there are many other things that Jesus did. If they*
> *were all written down one by one, I suppose that the whole*
> *world could not hold the books that would be written.*
> *(John 21:25)*

The Gospel of Mark has two endings. An ending universally accepted by Christianity stops abruptly with Mother Mary fleeing from the empty sepulcher to which Jesus had been brought after being taken down from the cross. The other more controversial ending, found only in some manuscripts and translations, contains a passing reference to the Ascension. In this alternative, Mark has Jesus appearing to the eleven disciples in Jerusalem as they were eating, whereupon he gives this fantastic message:

> *Go throughout the whole world and preach the gospel to*
> *all people. . . . Believers will be given the power to perform*
> *miracles: they will drive out demons in my name; they will*
> *speak in strange tongues; if they pick up snakes or drink any*

*poison, they will not be harmed; they will place their hands on
sick people, and these will get well.* (Mark 16:15, 17–18)

*After the Lord Jesus had talked with them, he was taken up
to heaven and sat at the right side of God.* (Mark 16:19)

The gospel according to Luke has a different version. Rather than
having Jesus rise to heaven from a Jerusalem eating hall, Luke
moves the final scene to the town of Bethany. First, Jesus appears
before his terrified disciples, easing their distress at seeing him
by having them feel his flesh and bones. Then he reminds them
of why he died:

*This is what is written: the Messiah must suffer and must
rise from death three days later. . . . You are witnesses of these
things. . . . Then he led them out of the city and as far as
Bethany, where he raised his hands and blessed them. As he
was blessing them, he departed from them and was taken up
into heaven.* (Luke 24:46, 48, 50–51)

Who was Luke? No one knows whether the person writing Luke
was named Luke. Or whether the author of the Matthew Gospel
was someone named Matthew. Or if there were a John and Mark
who were divinely inspired to write their biographies of Jesus
of Nazareth. If Jesus himself ever wrote a word, it has not been
preserved.

The omissions and conflicts are distressing because everything occurred in secret. Then, for generations, the stories were
retold orally by people having motive to exaggerate or lie in the
cause of establishing their new religion. The four Gospels are
believed to have been written between 35 and 150 years after the
crucifixion, but we cannot be sure. All four Gospels were written
in Greek, and contain extensive quotes from Jesus, spoken origi-
nally in Aramaic and then passed along orally for thirty-five or
more years. By who and to whom, no one knows.

If you were a juror asked to weigh such testimony and conduct in a trial determining the circumstances surrounding an
alleged Ascension to heaven, how would you vote?

Chapter Eighteen

S tudying the Bible can be an exhausting, even numbing, experience because the level of mayhem is so high. Beginning
with the Noah holocaust straight through to the crucifixion of
Jesus, the blood flows almost continuously. Early on, Abraham's
descendants are enslaved in Egypt for a nightmarish four hundred years. This epoch included the killing of all firstborn Hebrew
boys. Their subsequent freedom was purchased with nine brutish
miracles, including the killing of all Egyptian firstborn. God then
tried to prepare his chosen people for nationhood with a grueling
forty-year circular march that killed off an unfaithful older generation so that a new generation could inherit the Promised Land.

However, the Promised Land was already taken. Two hundred and fifty years of murderous warfare did not resolve the
question of ownership. In the meantime, a theocratic Hebrew
state experienced endless anarchy, which led to demands for
a strong king. The monarchy was then established, with some
positive early results during the first three reigns. Royal corruption led to hundreds of years of gruesome civil and foreign conflict, which ended only when a vigorous foreign empire smashed
Israel and exiled its people. More wars, the kingdom of Judah
was destroyed, and the Jews faced exile yet again. Waves of foreign conquests continued: Persian, Assyrian, Greek, and Roman.
God directed much of the conflict and cruelty himself, punishing
virtually all the Near East nations for various offenses.

The endless warring and civil savagery are numbing. God's
experiment with people produced too much ugliness, and if tort
lawyers existed at the dawn of time, God would have been sued
for product-defect liability in his creation of humankind. The Old
Testament went to final print with the prophecy that the end of
the world was coming because God wanted a fresh start, one in

which there would be no evil. In truth, God was unable to successfully manage the one small corner of the planet where Asia and Africa meet. His word does not deal with the other 90 percent of the planet. During these millennia, the Mayans, Fiji Islanders, Chinese, African tribes, Laplanders, and innumerable other groups and nations spread across the continents lived apparently uninspired and unmolested by him.

Who was responsible for all the killing? Much of it was by God himself:

> *You people have rejected me. . . . So I reached out and crushed you because I was tired of controlling my anger. . . . I destroyed you, my people, I killed your children because you did not stop your evil ways. There are more widows in your land than grains of sand by the sea. I killed your young men in their prime and made their mothers suffer. (Jer. 15:6–8)*

What God would say that? What person would? Presumably the wisest men in the Jewish nation determined that Jeremiah's "I killed your children" was an accurate proclamation from the Lord. Presumably, God inspired the final selections of scripture because, after all, only he could know as a certainty which words were his and which belonged to the many pretenders.

Whatever the process, the Lord and the wise men agreed that the Bible should forever inform the world that God once said, "I killed your children. . . . I killed your young men." But why? Why broadcast such a thing for eternity? The answer can only lie at the bottom of the divide between today's modern sensibilities and ancient tribal certainties about justice. In that remote world of twenty-five hundred years ago, God's killing of children and forcibly creating widowhood among suffering mothers was a natural part of life's nasty circle.

And the sins of the father were fiercely visited upon the family and later generations. That too was justice, Bible style. It was a time when some parents sacrificed their babies in burning flames to one god or another. We are shocked because many, if not most, ancient biblical notions of love, mercy, and justice conflict with our modern comprehension of these concepts and, therefore, seem cruel.

The world of old is *not* the world of contemporary Western sensibilities. The tribes and tribunes of the Middle East killed with a passion that is today the ethic of contemporary terrorists, *jihadis*, revenge warriors, beheaders, and 9/11 suicide fanatics. The Bible reveals the foundations of their world.

Recently, we saw in Afghanistan milder vestiges of ancient fundamentalist culture. It seemed incomprehensible that Taliban-style Islam required women to remain indoors behind darkened windows to avoid being seen or to be fully covered and male-escorted when leaving the house. Limbs were severed as punishment for certain crimes, and death by stoning was meted out in Kabul for alleged religious offenses. That was one version of the Koran come to life, one version of ancient desert tribal law still at work. Painful as it is to consider, in many respects, Taliban practices had Hebrew Bible counterparts:

> *If two men are having a fight and the wife of one tries to help her husband by grabbing hold of the other man's genitals, show her no mercy; cut off her hand. (Deut. 25:11–12)*

Or if one prefers there are the subtleties of the King James Version of the Bible:

> *When men strive together one with another, and the wife of the one draweth near for to deliver her husband out of the hand of him that smiteth him, and putteth forth her hand, and taketh him by the secrets: Then thou shalt cut off her hand, thine eye shall not pity her. (Deut. 25:11–12)*

Show no mercy, or pity, as the case may be. Whether written in Hebrew, Elizabethan English, or today's vernacular, that statute was legislated by God. Today, such a law seems both outrageous and silly. Yet, in certain Islamic countries, aside from the deposed Taliban, amputation remains a popular punishment. In biblical times, God's scriptural laws were accepted as the merciful commands of the Lord. To the tribal woman who grabbed the genitals of her husband's attacker, a hand amputation was merciful indeed compared to death by stoning. There are numerous other parallels between the ancient tribal codes. For example, we observe the Muslim practice among men of showing respect to God by wearing a beard. Some in the West find this custom bizarre, forgetting that the Old Testament commands devotion to God by the wearing of beard and side curls:

> *Do not cut the hair on the sides of your head or trim your beard. (Lev. 19:27–28)*

Presumably, Jesus followed most of the law and showed respect to God as commanded. Christianity later repealed most of the eternal law—retaining the Ten Commandments and some others—and then generally substituted its own exclusive law of salvation: follow Jesus or burn in a way equaling crucifixion in pain and horror, but incalculably worse because it continues until beyond the end of time. Jesus' cruel death lasted less than a day. Under traditional Christian teaching, even today, the majority of humanity is doomed to a fate worse than death. Indeed, during the era of early Christianity, more than 99 percent of all people on the planet were consigned to hell, having never even heard of Jesus.

If today God returned from the desert to intervene in our world, how would we know it? Yes, the Red Sea has again been parted, and we call it the Suez Canal. Jews again populate the Promised Land, or at least a tiny fraction of it, and through the ages, many wise men have spoken prophetic words that came true, words that have enriched and blessed our lives. Other men have proven to be false prophets—Marx and Hitler among the many.

The question remains: who speaks the truth from God?

The Lord's ancient messengers conducted their live broadcasts unaccompanied by flashes of lightning, trumpets, or bands of angels. Their listeners would have been right to wonder, "Is this guy from God or not?"

Has the Lord sent no great messages for nearly two thousand years? Or by Islamic reckoning, for 1,400 years? Has all wisdom from the past 1,400 or more years been free of divine inspiration?

Have all the incredible history-making events for two millennia reflected only mankind's random efforts?

No. Evidence, wisdom, and faith strongly compel the conclusion that certain remarkable changes in the lives of God's children bear a miraculous design. We are surrounded by it but see little. This will become clearer. To assist in recognizing the divine, it is useful to continue peering back at the world from whence came our scriptures. Ancient darkness has the ironic effect of shedding necessary light on the future.

The Jesus legend grew in size and intensity. Its foremost proponent was a Jew born as Saul, but who became Paul from Tarsus, which is now in Turkey. Many give Paul the title of founder of Christianity because his Herculean efforts in developing and spreading the new theology did much to establish its permanent base in the Mediterranean world. Moreover, Paul's doctrinal contributions to Christian theology equal or exceed those of Jesus. All of Jesus' words reported in the Bible may be given in one oration of about three hours.

Paul's numerous letters to early Christian churches in Greece, Turkey, and other Mediterranean outposts form the earliest Christian scripture. Commonly referred to as epistles, the letters date from perhaps twenty-five years following the crucifixion and announce the new church's principal doctrines. Paul was a star in his time. He was also a man of excesses in brilliance, fanaticism, torment of the soul, and messianic faith.

Ironically, Paul, the intellectual fountain of Christianity, began his religious leadership as a fanatic persecutor of Christians:

> *You have been told how I used to live when I was devoted to the Jewish religion, how I persecuted without mercy the [Christian] church and did my best to destroy it. . . . But God in his grace chose me even before I was born, and called me to serve him. (Gal. 1:13–15)*

Thus, Paul claims he was chosen before birth to do God's work. If so, he attributes to God his mission first as a fanatic Jew prosecuting Christians "without mercy," and then as a Christian fanatically developing and spreading the new word. Experience teaches, however, that great caution is appropriate when receiving messages from fanatics. Usually, we politely ignore such people.

Fired up and messianic, Paul was potent in getting out the message of faith, and it evolved into theology under his leadership. Central to the message was the Jewish prophetic news broadcast by Jesus: the apocalypse is near. Indeed, Paul never married, contending it was useless for him to do so since the end was imminent.

Paul preached during the generation following the death of Christ, and the historical setting was still very ancient. The Jews remained an oppressed people under Roman domination. It was 1,900 years ago, and in a part of the world hardly modern even for its day.

It was a time when Jupiter, chief of the Roman gods, was the reigning deity of the heavens. For Paul, however, there was a ground war against sin, and he was the commanding general. Evil was the enemy, and it was everywhere aggressive. Paul saw a pitched battle underway with terrible demons working hard to undo mankind and angels busy doing the work of God. Paul's mission was to lead the forces of good by wielding the teachings of Christ to slay demons, Satan, and sin. This was a powerful man bringing white hot urgency to faith.

Paul's vision of omnipresent sin included the hateful sin enslaving his own being. The genius behind Christianity confusingly describes himself as a tortured soul in which evil operates his being:

> *I am a mortal, sold as a slave to sin. I do not understand what I do; for I don't do what I like to do, but instead I do what I hate. . . . I am not really the one who does this thing; rather, it is the sin that lives in me. I know that good does not live in me, I am not able to do it. I don't do the good I want to do; instead, I do the evil that I do not want to do. If I do what I don't want to do, this means that I am no longer the one who does it; instead, it is the sin that lives in me. (Rom. 7:14–20)*

These are the words of a man in torment. Apostle Paul is anguished over the sin possessing his body. He is a hostage, a man captive to warring emotions and imaginings. Paul reads today as if the wrenching pain in his soul still holds sway 1,900 years after his personal battles with the devil gave impetus and form to New Testament revelations. Thus, the Bible tells of the apostle's raging struggle with the tenth commandment, which warns against desire for a neighbor's possessions. To Paul, the mere mention of the word "desire" fired up his sinful desires and even led to his spiritual death. Paul is a troubled man, and he provides an extraordinary window into his soul:

> Shall we say, then, that the [Mosaic] Law itself is sinful? Of course not! But it was the law that made me know what sin is. If the law had not said, "Do not desire what belongs to someone else," I would not have known such a desire. But by means of that commandment sin found its chance to stir up all kinds of selfish desires in me. . . . And the commandment which was meant to bring life, in my case brought death. Sin found its chance, and by means of the commandment it deceived me and killed me. (Rom. 7:7–11)

Thus, for Paul, the cherished wisdom of the tenth commandment brought spiritual death. Paul's body cannot resist desire. He was

> a prisoner of the law of sin which is at work in my body. What an unhappy man I am!" (Rom. 7:23–24).

Understandably, a man so tormented by sin would ground his theology in the great battle to defeat it. Paul's personal torment became the engine of Christianity, pushing all forward to slay the beast of sin. Perhaps it is time to consider whether his personal nightmare from two millennia ago should forever hold people hostage. Paul's trench warfare of the soul may need a ceasefire. Perhaps it is time to permit the light of a newer message to shine through.

Successfully spreading the new message required Paul's persistence. The early Christian congregations in Turkey thought the Mosaic Code should be preserved as part of the amended religion spreading under Jesus' name. Paul said no: only faith in Jesus, faith alone, is needed to put people right with God:

> [W]e know that a person is put right with God only through faith in Jesus Christ, never by doing what the Law requires. . . . But if a person is put right with God through the Law, it means that Christ died for nothing! (Gal. 2:16, 21)

> [W]hen the right time finally came, God sent his own Son. He came as the son of a human mother and lived under the Jewish Law, to redeem those who were under the Law, so that we might become God's children. . . . So then, you are no longer a slave but a child. And since you are his child, God will give you all that he has for his children. (Gal. 4:4–5, 7)

Paul was insistent that none of the Hebrew law be followed. Thus, if a man was circumcised under the Mosaic Code, then he was also circumcised from the Church:

> Once more I warn any man who allows himself to be circumcised that he is obliged to obey the whole [Mosaic] Law. Those of you who try to put yourself right with God by obeying the law have cut yourselves off from Christ. You are outside God's grace. (Gal. 5:3–4)

Paul's abandonment of the law seems to stretch well beyond Jesus' teaching. Jesus had indeed criticized parts of the ancient law. For example, he taught that Judaism's many dietary laws wrongly made what went into one's mouth more important than what came out. Nevertheless, Jesus still supported the Mosaic Code:

> Do not think that I have come to do away with the Law of Moses and the teachings of the prophets. I have not come to do away with them, but to make their teachings come true. (Matt. 5:17)

Here was the great divide opening between Judaism and apostle Paul's theology of Christianity. Judaism was a law-obsessed religion, 613 commandments from God covering life's every breath.

Follow those laws and you followed God's will. God would love and reward you for conduct becoming a servant of God. Those laws, declared eternal by the Lord, were still central to the Judaism of Jesus. Paul, however, revoked the law for Christ's followers and substituted faith in its place. Thus, a powerful, blind faith in Jesus and God was the new duty of the Lord's followers. The Jews had it wrong, Paul said:

> *Because they did not depend on faith but on what they did.*
> *(Rom. 9:32)*

Instead of 613 rules to guide one's life to good conduct, Paul insisted there was but one commandment from God, to love your neighbor, because doing so will sweep away all harm:

> *The commandments, "Do not commit adultery; do not commit murder; do not steal; do not desire what belongs to someone else"—all these, and any others besides, are summed up in the one command, "Love your neighbor as you love yourself." If you love others, you will never do them wrong; to love, then is to obey the whole Law. (Rom. 13:9–10)*

Paul is right. In a world in which each man truly loved his neighbor, wrongful conduct would disappear. The law of love would imprison evil. However, Paul wasn't ministering for the long term, and Paul wasn't realistic. Like Jesus, Paul's urging to "love your neighbor and defeat evil" was broadcast in a world about to end. The apocalypse is coming because evil had won. For Paul, Christianity is the light in a dark night whose chorus of groans soon would end:

> *[W]e know that up to the present time all of creation groans with pain, like the pain of childbirth. But it is not just creation alone which groans; we who have the Spirit as the first of God's gifts also groan within ourselves as we wait for God to make us his children and set our whole being free. (Rom. 8:22–23)*

[B]ecause you know that the time has come for you to wake up from your sleep. For the moment when we will be saved is closer now than it was when we first believed. The night is nearly over, day is almost here. (Rom. 13:1–12)

For Apostle Paul, as with Jesus, the world was inhabited by an active devil seeking to take control of bodies by filling them with sin, but with the coming end, combat with the devil is almost over. So love each other now and be right in God's glory.

If times have changed beyond imagining since the days of the apostle, is a changed message also beyond imagining? "Love your neighbor" is a commandment that never stopped a tyrant from warring with his neighbor. Surely, the Lord has more imagination and wisdom than to stay with the tried and *un*true. Faith and evidence suggest something newer is in the air.

Was the Jesus/Paul message intended only as a short-term program? Why not decree it forever as the answer to worldly woe? Because it cannot work. It was not expected to work. Recall the Bible's first covenant, made between God and Noah:

Never again will I put the earth under a curse because of what people do; I know that from the time they are young their thoughts are evil. . . . I promise that never again will all living beings be destroyed. (Gen. 8:21, 9:15)

Evil thoughts are part of humankind. Some may overcome them, but the truth of history is that evil has not been extinguished and the sin-bashing message of Jesus and Paul has not provided the cure. Jesus and Paul preached the apocalypse was coming because the world's evil was more than God could tolerate. Shattering the planet is very, very serious business. Hundreds of millions would die even in ancient times. If there were any chance that loving your neighbor or carrying your enemy's pack or offering your right cheek for more pain would end evil, then the apocalypse would be unnecessary.

If sin could be defeated through faith, the end of the world could be canceled by God, and happily so. If good was to triumph through the message of Christ, then the awful time of horror need never arrive. Hell could be closed and left a vacant slum.

But the Jewish/Christian message of apocalypse was never canceled. It was repeated to the last book of the New Testament because evil was winning, and love was wanting. Even an omnipotent God could offer no long-term solution other than ending the world and beginning anew. How sad. Because so little time remained, Paul even recommended against married love because doomsday was too near:

> *What I mean, my friends is this: there is not much time left, and from now on married people should live as though they were not married. (1 Cor. 7:29)*

Married people should live as though they were not married? What a bizarre sense of urgency and emergency. If this instruction was followed, the planet would have been depopulated in fifty years, and the self-made apocalypse complete. Yet, that remains scripture even today because the Bible is cast in divine stone. It has never been amended.

In other respects, however, the Christian world would become easier because of its post-Jesus repeal of the Mosaic Code. There would be an end to restrictive dietary laws. For the men, the circumcision ritual was over. How powerful an idea that must have been in a patriarchic epoch with primitive medicine! Repealing the law also meant no more daily animal sacrifices and offerings to the priesthood. Inconvenient rules of all kinds could be ignored: men no longer had to bathe after a discharge or women during menstruation. Paul's Christianity was a welcome parole for the legally oppressed. It is understandable that replacing the harsh bindings of the Old Testament's Mosaic Code with a regimen of private personal faith won many followers. Since the end was near, the new temporary burdens of faith and goodness would be light.

Paul's Christianity also provided a revolutionary response to sin: easy forgiveness. Whereas the Mosaic Code specified complicated animal offerings for absolution from petty sins and death for the many serious offenses, Paul's message was remarkably simple: forgiveness through faith in Jesus. Under the Jewish covenant with God, the laws controlled, but Apostle Paul preached that Jesus gave his life so that a new covenant could be born:

> *In order to set us free from this present evil age, Christ gave himself for our sins, in obedience to the will of our God and Father. (Gal. 1:4)*

If you do not believe this is God's new way, says, Paul:

> *[M]ay [you] be condemned to hell! (Gal. 1:9)*

Paul and Jesus were warriors against evil. Religion itself is a natural human response to the problem of evil. The Bible tells us that Adam and Eve were undone by evil. Jesus and Paul accepted the Garden of Eden explanation of the birth of evil and preached its truth as God's word. Their shared vision of the world was that rampant evil was finally to be defeated by the apocalypse.

However, they were wrong; rampant evil will ultimately be defeated only by universal liberty. When the unfree in every tyrant's dark corner believe in and then exercise their inalienable rights in an effective constitutional framework, liberty will have a universal chance. Only then can massive evil finally be checked.

Chapter Nineteen

The Old Testament God was young. Perhaps the role of father to all humanity was too severe a test too soon for the youthful universe maker. Mankind is often foolish, disobedient, untruthful, aggressive, and cruel. Such children would try any father's patience. The truth is, God as a new father made many and serious mistakes. It takes time to get it right.

With age and maturity, the Lord assertedly fathered a son, Jesus, to be his messenger for the news that God had changed his mind: the eternal law was repealed and not eternal and that God wanted many more children than merely the chosen few. Now, anyone could be his son by declaring faith. So serious was this more mature Lord that he elected to sacrifice his son as the down payment on the new covenant. The apostle Paul told in the most fanciful way how this would come about:

> God will take back with Jesus those who have died believing in him. . . . There will be the shout of command, the archangel's voice, the sound of God's trumpet, and the Lord himself will come down from heaven. Those who have died believing in Christ will rise to life first; then we who are living at that time will be gathered up along with them in the clouds to meet the Lord in the air. (1 Thess. 4:14–17)

To Paul, it is true beyond any question that the God of the New Testament is just. However, justice delayed is not justice denied because Paul's justice of flaming fire and destruction was to wait until after the apocalypse:

> God will do what is right: he will bring suffering on those who make you suffer, and he will give relief to you who suffer. . . . He will do this when the Lord Jesus appears from

heaven with his mighty angels, with a flaming fire, to punish those who reject God and do not obey the Good News about our Lord Jesus. They will suffer the punishment of eternal destruction, separated from the presence of the Lord and from his glorious might. (2 Thess. 1:6–9)

The question we must consider is whether this "new" scripture, now some 1,800 years old, is the final word of God. Or has God grown wiser?

Clearly, Paul's telling of the revealed message to have faith through Christ or suffer the punishment of eternal destruction is a merciless casting of fate. The vast majority of people who have ever lived on this earth, even today, do not exercise faith through Jesus. Billions and billions of Hindus, Buddhists, Muslims, Jews, atheists, animists, and others are thus consigned to the "punishment of eternal destruction." It is a cruel revelation that demands faith or assigns hell.

It is also a bizarre revelation that posits fanciful struggles involving deadly wickedness, as told by Paul. When a church in Thessalonica, Greece, came to believe Christ had already returned from heaven, Paul wrote to correct the error. The world will learn of Christ's nearness, Paul says, when the battle between good and evil reaches a crescendo. Then a strange struggle will follow, pitting the chief of evil known as the wicked one against Christ:

At the proper time the Wicked One will appear. The Mysterious Wickedness is already at work. . . . Then the Wicked One will be revealed, but when the Lord Jesus comes, he will kill him with the breath from his mouth and destroy him with his dazzling presence. The Wicked One will come with the power of Satan and perform all kinds of false miracles and wonders, and use every kind of wicked deceit on those who will perish. (2 Thess. 2:6–10)

Christ had earlier exorcised demons, overcome the devil in a mountaintop face-off, and in the ultimate postmortem, will dazzle to death Satan's stand-in. All the heavenly bodies will burn, and only righteousness will dwell in mankind's heart. The New Testament is powerful theology. It is miraculous stuff. Again, however, it was theology made on a lost bet that the world was soon coming to an end.

Moreover, it was a theology in an epoch when few could read. Newspapers, magazines, TV, movies, radio, telephones, and computers were major miracles in the unimaginably distant future. Thus, the Bible focuses on prophets, real and fake, male and female, because they were the broadcasters of their day. Indeed, Jesus was welcomed as a prophet; even the 7th century Koran describes him as such.

The irony is powerful: we continue to hold sacred the texts of that ancient and unknowable world even as we shun all else about it and even as we fight the terrorists still locked within its remnants.

One final look at the world we left behind.

The final book of the New Testament is called the Revelation to John. It was written at a time when the early Christians were being persecuted for their faith. Apostle John was told to write everything down and then to send the resulting book to churches suffering persecution in seven Greek cities. The revelations came to John from an other-worldly being described as:

> *[A] human being wearing a robe that reached to his feet, and a gold band around his chest. His hair was white as wool . . . and his eyes blazed like fire; his feet shone like brass . . . and his voice sounded like a roaring waterfall. (Rev. 1:13–15)*

We do not know who the strange revealer was, but John sent the messages as instructed. One of the seven was directed to the church in the city of Thyatira. In it, John showed ferocious contempt for the church's immorality in tolerating Jezebel, and he promised horrific punishment and death. It was repent or die:

> *You tolerate that woman Jezebel, who calls herself a messenger of God. By her teaching she misleads my servants into practicing sexual immorality and eating food that has been*

*offered to idols. . . . And so I will throw her on a bed where
she and those who have committed adultery with her will suffer terribly . . . unless they will repent. . . . I will also kill her
followers. (Rev. 2:20–23)*

This is scripture armed for battle. If you follow others rather than
Jesus or sin badly in priestly eyes, you will be killed. This is
indeed a rough message from the Lord and reminiscent of God's
Old Testament tactics in enforcing obedience to his law. It is a
version of the eternal message "be good or die." It would appear
the Lord remained unhinged by the presence of evil and its power
over people. The world had to end to finally vanquish evil.

John's Revelation also includes otherworldly whimsy, fantastic visions beyond reality. His work, God's word, is bizarre.
John reveals he saw an angel blow a trumpet, causing a star to fall
to earth, and out of the smoke there came locusts:

*The locusts looked like horses ready for battle; on their
heads they had what seemed to be crowns of gold, and their
faces were like human faces. Their hair was like women's hair,
their teeth were like lion's teeth. . . . They have tails and stings
like those of a scorpion, and it is with their tails that they have
the power to hurt people for five months. (Rev. 9:7–8, 10)*

Stars falling to earth and locusts looking like horses are part of
the tableau of an ancient world that bequeathed the word, saying
its truths must remain unchallenged for all time. Are such visions
still to hold us fast? Does God's word in the time of locusts really
reflect his last message? May we consider the possibility that an
older, wiser God may have updated his message since the time of
John's revelations? Unless there is new scripture, the old remains
as an often frightening museum of disturbing visions. These are
the last visions we see, because the Bible then closes.

God's scriptures remain unaltered even today. When you
place your left hand on the Bible and swear to tell the whole truth,
you are in touch with the awful horror and the wicked one, the
darkest forces of evil that still roam the pages of the Holy Book.

Today, however, the more realistic danger is that mankind, rather than an earth-shattering Lord will destroy the world - Armageddon. If so, it will arrive because evil men possessed the means to inflict great death and proceeded by evil impulse to do it. The twin messages of the New Testament, to love others as we love ourselves and have faith in Jesus/God, are very decent. However, they failed to prevent the innumerable massive evils of the past two millennia.

The New Testament's message about governance had especially tragic consequences. While Jesus taught that it was sinful for a man even to contemplate relations with a woman not his wife, the occupying Romans killed at will in the Near East and elsewhere. Then and now, immense evil came from tribes and nations in the thrall of deadly leaders.

In Paul's letter to the Romans, he writes that civil authorities exist only with God's permission. Therefore, obeying authority is obeying God's plan. More harm than can be imagined derives from this message of divine sanction and blind obedience:

> *Everyone must obey state authorities, because no authority exists without God's permission, and God has put the existing authorities there. Whoever opposes the existing authority opposes what God has ordered; and anyone who does so will bring judgment on himself. For rulers are not to be feared by those who do good, but by those who do evil. Would you like to be unafraid of those in authority? Then do what is good, and they will praise you, because they are God's servants working for your own good. . . . For this reason you must obey the authority—not just because of God's punishment, but also as a matter of conscience. (Rom. 13:1–5)*

No authority exists without God's permission, says New Testament scripture. It is difficult to imagine a political-science lesson more wrong than apostle Paul's. His assessment that those who govern are "God's servants working for your own good" is foolish in the best of eras and unimaginable when despotism reigns.

Common sense suggests that Paul's letter was a calculated effort to please Roman authorities who were then persecuting Christians. Happy is he who is persecuted? Apparently not. Worse, Paul's statement that "whoever opposes the existing authority opposes what God has ordered" was a travesty that became the tragedy known as the divine right of kings.

Paul's teaching that only evil persons need fear authority ignores this fact: Jesus had been doing "what is good" when Pilate, the existing authority and presumably one of God's servants, crucified Jesus rather than "praise" his good works. John the Baptist, the greatest man ever, according to Jesus, had been decapitated by Herod for preaching against incest. Surely, Paul, a man doing "what is good," was the victim of his own untruth: he was persecuted, imprisoned, tortured, and executed by the Roman state authorities.

Were the killing Romans "God's servants working for [Paul's] own good"? Rome did not praise Paul for his good works. It killed him and countless other Christians. The list of horrific despots is lengthier than one can bear, and surely, their murderous reigns were not with God's permission.

The evil that men pronounce long outlives them, and the church's adoption of Paul's divine permission for governing authority had a long and inglorious run of nearly 1,600 years. Murder, mayhem, and oppression of every kind have been committed under cover of Apostle Paul's pen, assertedly inspired by God and still in the Holy Bible.

Without an amendment, God's word continues forever untouched by the lessons of time. Does anyone today believe that "no authority exists without God's permission"? Probably not. Tyrants from Herod to Hitler were instruments of mass evil. They are among the innumerable madmen who have tortured and killed their way across history's stage, and by their hands, guns, and gas hundreds of millions have perished. Paul cannot have been right.

Wouldn't God want to set the official record straight?

The Bible still contains scripture that would send to hell all the good and brave people who opposed evil authority, oppression, or authoritarian violence. Are the American rebels against authority, among them Thomas Jefferson and George Washington, burning there? If no one believes "this" anymore or "that" anymore, when does the term "abandonment" begin to apply?

Surely, no one today believes God pre-approves all governments or that all governments should be blindly obeyed. The task of saying so fell to Thomas Jefferson in 1776, who wrote these inspired words in the revolutionary scripture of liberty:

> *That whenever any Form of Government becomes destructive of these [unalienable rights], it is the Right of the People to alter or abolish it. (Declaration of Independence)*

God's divine intervention in the eighteenth century—if we have the faith to believe it—was long delayed in coming but still effective in repealing Paul's blessing of all civil authority. In the most important transformation in two millennia, *the divine right of kings was replaced by the divine right to liberty.* This is modern scripture.

Ancient scriptural revelations are preoccupied with one corner of the planet. It is doubtful that evil and sin dwelt only in the Near East, but because the Bible is locked in time and place, God's word doesn't display the fabric of life in other lands now called China, Australia, Mexico, Canada, and Congo.

If there is one God, then he must have been everywhere tending to his flock. Fathers, mothers, and children in ancient Peru arose each morning to the same sun that nine hours earlier had warmed the Jerusalem temple where priests made their daily animal sacrifices. The streets of Jerusalem were filled with people hawking wares and prophecies just as Chinese communities daily came to commercial life with artisans and rice growers. Eskimos went out to fish even as Jesus recruited fishermen. Mothers kissed their babies goodnight in India as Herod's soldiers sliced apart babies in Bethlehem.

The world is so much larger than the dusty backyard in which Moses and Jesus prayed out their lives. Did God not love the Eskimos too? Were these Artic Circle innocents to die in the awful horror because ten thousand miles away Near Eastern tribes sinned beyond God's level of tolerance? Their great spirit told them otherwise. So we may rightly ask, "Who owns the truth?" Following the death of Jesus, Japan's ancient farmers labored on in ignorance of their hideous fate. Their contemporary, one Paul of faraway Tarsus, preached the message that nonbelievers were destined for a fire-baked hell because they knew not Jesus. Of course, the rice farmers on Hokkaido Island had never heard of him, nor had Paul any knowledge of the divine power to whom the Japanese prayed for a meaningful life and comprehensible death. The one God had not revealed to Fiji Islanders what Jesus and Paul knew of heavenly salvation.

In fact, Paul lived in a world 99 percent pagan and unfortunately for them, God's new message was that pagans needed Jesus for their heavenly salvation. Is it merciful for a universal God to tell only a few the secret of eternity and burn the rest? Are not all people to be cherished? Can there be only one kind of rewarded love in a world God made endlessly diverse?

There are many saintly souls in all four corners of the planet, or now that we know the earth is round, in all latitudes and longitudes. Divine earthly blessings are for all good people regardless of their religious faith, or nonfaith.

Chapter Twenty

Conventional wisdom and language hold that Judaism, Christianity, and Islam are three distinct religions. Yet all three worship the same Father, the God who inexplicably selected Abraham to establish monotheism. All believers want to do as their Lord asks, and surely he asks the same of all. Can there be three distinct religions among the faithful of the same God? Certainly there are doctrinal and procedural differences—Christ's asserted divinity for one—but if all three congregations direct their prayers to the same Father, then to how many faiths is that Father really ministering?

Consider that each morning the pope arises and prays to Allah. He does. Yahweh, the Lord, and Allah are aliases of the one God. "Allah" simply means "God" in Arabic. All prayer goes to a central receiving point, and all divine gifts are distributed from there. If the leaders of Israel and Palestine pray at all, they seek divine guidance from the same Father. We can envision him listening to the eternal squabbling over what constitutes sin, which cleansing acts will wash it away, who earns passage to heaven, and how the world will finally end. Such debates must drive the Lord to distraction, but it should not distract from the central truth of one God for all three major faiths.

Thus, one critical purpose of the Final Testament is to return the three sibling faiths to their Father's table in peace and allow them to sit together, reading from the same book. How sad that for millennia Christians, Jews, and Muslims served up death at their family disunions. Father must have cried. He must be crying still.

However, the observation that three religious siblings adore the same Father does not imply naïveté. It is simply true. The divine answer lies in having an empowered faithful keep murderous men from power while watching carefully that good people stay the course. Life will always have its mountains to climb, and some will fall making the effort. Nevertheless, through the millennia, mass evil has been the legacy of unrestrained power exercised by rogue men of all descriptions: kings, Caesars, tribal leaders, dynasty rulers, priests, generals, chiefs, dictators, authoritarians, despots, and warlords. Whatever the label, their cravings for domination have caused untold loss of life. How refreshing, then, to consider that religion may have a new direction: the universal victory of ordinary good people over tyrants.

Faith is belief without proof. New writings may become canonized scripture if we have faith in their divinity. Faith is not a matter in which government has a say; it is from the people and for the people. Perhaps it's an instinct, or perhaps it is like air, something we must breathe in order to live. For all time, humans have held beliefs despite the absence of hard evidence. Atheists may snicker and laugh it off as silliness, but even they must admit that faith has endured and will endure.

It would seem far better, therefore, to be welcoming rather than hostile to the idea that across the millennia, a powerful God does refreshingly great things from time to time in order to reflect the changed longings of the faithful. Do we really want to believe God became disengaged and fell silent nearly two thousand years ago after wrongly revealing a coming time of horror?

In 1776, the world changed profoundly. In declaring independence, the fledgling American nation redefined humanity's status on earth and its relationship with God. The Revolutionary War and struggles that followed it sought to prove that right makes might. The Constitution drafted in 1787 was as strikingly original in its time as anything Moses carried down from Mount Sinai. Moreover, whereas much of the Bible remains an incomprehensible mystery, the Federalist Papers were written to make sure that the new charter was well understood by those receiving it.

Can the Declaration of Independence, the Constitution of the United States, and *The Federalist* be canonized as scripture? Yes, if we have faith.

What then is scripture? It is anything that God inspired, said, wrote, sang, recited, shouted, or ordered broadcast. The earliest Bible, or Old Testament, did not spring into existence as a complete scripture. There was no publishing event announcing the Bible to a waiting world. Rather, over the course of centuries scrolls were written, passed along, unfurled for tribal readings, and eventually collected by priests. Then at some point, the most influential rabbis formally recognized certain of the many ancient scrolls as God's true word, as the Hebrew Bible. The New Testament underwent a similar but much abbreviated effort, spanning about three hundred years from Paul's first letters to the final canonization of the Christian New Testament.

The priests' undertaking of these early efforts remained open to all forms of holy writ be it humane, profane, or all that lies between. Biblical verse is often eccentric. By comparison, to modern eyes the inspired revolutionary writings of eighteenth-century American colonials seem more scriptural than the ancient real thing. The real thing? Scripture includes home-maintenance procedures for mildew problems sent by the Lord:

> *If any of you find that the Lord has sent mildew on your house, then you must go and tell the priest about it. The priest shall order everything to be moved out of the house before he goes to examine the mildew. . . . If there are greenish or reddish spots that are eating the wall, he shall leave the house and lock it up for seven days. (Lev. 14:35–38)*

Scripture includes the questionable wisdom that male births are cleaner than female births:

> *For seven days after a woman gives birth to a son, she is ritually unclean, as she is during her monthly period. . . . For fourteen days after a woman gives birth to a daughter, she is ritually unclean, as she is during her monthly period. (Lev. 12:1, 5)*

Scripture includes home dermatological remedies:

> *If there is a white sore on your skin which turns the hairs*

white and is full of pus, it is a chronic skin disease. . . . If any of you have a boil that has healed and if afterward a white swelling or a reddish-white spot appears . . . you shall go to the priest. (Lev. 13:10, 18–19)

Scripture includes dietary laws prescribing locusts:

You may eat locusts, crickets, or grasshoppers. But all other small things that have wings and also crawl must be considered unclean. (Lev. 11:22–23)

Scripture includes the punishment of burning at the stake:

If a priest's daughter becomes a prostitute, she disgraces her father; she shall be burned to death. (Lev. 21:9)

Scripture includes God's command for the mass killing of women and children via serial holocausts:

But when you capture cities in the land your God is giving you, kill everyone. Completely destroy all the people: the Hittites, the Amorites, the Canaanites, the Perizzites, the Hivites, and the Jebusites. . . . Kill them, so that they will not make you sin against the Lord by teaching you to do all the disgusting things that they do in the worship of their gods. (Deut. 20:16–18)

Scripture includes a required manicure and shave for beautiful women captives:

When the Lord your God gives you victory in battle and you take prisoners, you may see among them a beautiful woman that you like and want to marry. Take her to your home where she will shave her head, cut her fingernails, and change her clothes. . . . Since you forced her to have intercourse with you, you cannot treat her as a slave and sell her. (Deut. 21:10–14)

Clearly, Holy Scripture is an open book; therefore, why not include the documents of the American Revelation? Are we not far more comfortable with them than with the just-recited Holy Scripture? Should we have holocaust material in motels and churches or the remarkable, inspired essays of *The Federalist* penned by Madison, Hamilton, and Jay?

If the Declaration of Independence, the Constitution, and *The Federalist* are adopted as scripture by Christianity, Islam, and Judaism, these wayward branches of monotheism would revere the same holy book or at least share the same final chapter of their sacred texts. The Bill of Rights would be the subject of sermon and prayer in New York, Baghdad, and Hong Kong. That would surely be cause for worldwide celebration.

The hope is that modern theology will teach that all humans are created equal in their possession of divine and inalienable rights, that those who rule are caretakers of limited powers granted for the purpose of protecting the rights and happiness of the people. Then, when their limited terms are up, the elected are to leave quietly so that mass evil has no chance to take hold. If religion will accept these principles, then evil power will be checked, and when universally applied, mass evil will be in checkmate.

The symbol for all this is not a cross upon which a tortured man is dying, but the Statue of Liberty, whose bright light is a beacon for the living.

What is faith? Faith demands only an act of will. Martin Luther said, "To have a god is nothing else than to trust and believe him with our whole heart," since "it is the trust and faith of the heart alone that makes both God and idol." Having faith is to trust and believe in something with your whole heart.

Most people would probably agree that if there is a God, then his inspiration was at work at liberty's birth in America. Nothing handed down during the past fourteen hundred years comes even close to the Declaration of Independence and the Constitution of the United States as tablets bearing God's inspiration. From the powerful truths of those documents, freedom has rolled around the world, allowing billions of people to experience lives of liberty rather than oppression.

What an extraordinary possibility that in 1776 God's ancient call for the world's end was finally replaced by a call for universal liberty and evil's end.

PART THREE

THE FINAL
TESTAMENT

Chapter Twenty-one

The Declaration of Independence

Four score and seven years ago our fathers brought forth on this continent, a new nation, conceived in Liberty, and dedicated to the proposition that all men are created equal.
—Abraham Lincoln, 1863

Thomas Jefferson was born on April 13, 1743, at Shadwell, a tobacco plantation in the Blue Ridge Mountains of Virginia. Jesus was born in Bethlehem, Judea, on an unknown date and year around 5 BC. Jefferson's family was distinguished in the colony, and the young man's brilliant mind was nurtured through disciplined education and cultural involvement. Jesus' family perhaps included God and a stepfather descended from Adam. At birth, he was exiled to Egypt because his protection from royal assassination could not be assured. To say the least, Jesus and Jefferson began their lives in different universes.

Jefferson was seventeen, tall and freckled, with blue-gray eyes and reddish hair, when he entered college. After two years at William and Mary, he spent five years as a student in the law office of George Wythe. The young lawyer read widely and deeply, steeping himself in the Greek and Latin classics as well as the works of the great philosophers, historians, and poets. He read French and Italian, studied German, and immersed himself in the natural sciences.

Jesus was probably unable to read and write, though he became very learned in the Hebrew Bible. His appearance is unknown, except for the likelihood that he had the aspect of a Near East tribesman, and wore a beard and side curls in accordance with Mosaic Law. Jesus was a magnetic figure, possessed a brilliant mind, and developed a dramatic flair for preaching. However, aside from a visit to the Jewish temple as a precocious twelve-year-old, nothing else is known of Jesus' life from birth until about his thirty-third year.

Jefferson showed an exceptional capacity for hard work. The young Virginian's sharp mind became disciplined, skeptical, and critical in matters of history, science, and social theories. He played the violin, danced, flirted, mingled at coffee houses, and paid close attention to the rebellious speeches of his day. In 1767, at the age of twenty-four, he was admitted to the bar, and in the years preceding the American Revolution, developed a very successful legal practice, frequently appearing before the highest court in the colony. All the while, Thomas Jefferson was given to philosophical conversations with the best and the wisest in Virginia, from whom he learned much during an era when discussions of liberty and justice were part of every engaging dinner.

In 1769, at the age of twenty-six, Thomas Jefferson began his political career in the Virginia House of Burgesses. In his first session there, he attempted to make it legally possible for owners to emancipate their slaves. He did not succeed, Jefferson tells us, because nothing liberal could succeed under the dominating British crown of King George III and his ruling ministers. The colonies' complaints against the monarchy were many. Lists of grievances were often the subject of petitions to the king, and in one of them Jefferson wrote:

> *[T]he God who gave us life gave us liberty at the same time; the hand of force may destroy but cannot disjoin them.*

Liberty and life were as one, divinely received and inseparable. These words began the American Revelation.

In the 1770s, the thirteen British colonies in America were home to fewer than three million persons. Fewer people than today live in Los Angeles or Chicago. Yet in the colonies' time of great stress, when the divine right of kings was still being exercised, a select group of men came to resist the loss of liberty.

Their remarkable talent, character, faith, and intelligence changed the world. The group included George Washington, Thomas Jefferson, James Madison, Samuel Adams, Benjamin Franklin, and Alexander Hamilton in the first rank and an extraordinary supporting group as well. Familiarly known as the Founding Fathers, these wise men came together from a small population in a still-remote part of the world to form what was surely the wisest group of governing men ever.

The Bible is filled with extraordinary individuals from Moses to Jesus, from King David to the apostle Paul, but nowhere in the Bible or elsewhere has such a group of remarkable men assembled for one historic moment, and together in the public glare brilliantly redefined man's historic status with God and country. Because they might die in the cause, the Founding Fathers agreed

> *with a firm reliance on the protection of Divine Providence, we mutually pledge to each other our Lives, our Fortunes and our sacred Honor. (Declaration of Independence)*

The goal was liberty. The enterprise for this pledge was history's first successful republic. They were revolutionaries dissolving political bands pulled too tight by an unyielding monarch. They sought the "equal station" God had entitled to all. Written by Thomas Jefferson, the Declaration of Independence begins:

> *When in the Course of human events it becomes necessary for one people to dissolve the political bands which have connected them with another, and to assume among the powers of the earth, the separate and equal station to which the Laws of Nature and of Nature's God entitles them.*

In 1775, armed conflict began in Massachusetts. Boston was both the center for colonial resistance and the headquarters of King George's troops. Nearby Lexington and Concord were early battle sites familiar to many Americans. These skirmishes pitted local militia against the world's most formidable military power. The battles, which drew first blood between king and colony, were the angry rumblings of those who felt oppressed and voiceless in the face of denied petitions.

The colonies had taken care to specify their grievances against the unyielding king, but he refused to accept or pass laws requested by the colonies, obstructed the administration of justice, cut off trade, dissolved legislatures, obstructed lawmaking, imposed taxes without consent, denied trial by jury, imposed military power over civil authority, quartered the military among the people, abolished needed laws, plundered shipping, and waged war against the colonies.

The abuses by King George were many and the history of unrestrained power has never been otherwise. It is not surprising, then, that God was pleased to inspire revolution against the British crown. In the Bible, the Lord had warned the Hebrews that kings do evil:

> *This is how your king will treat you. . . . He will make soldiers of your sons; some of them will serve in his war chariots, others in his cavalry, and others will run before his chariots. . . . Your sons will have to plow his fields, harvest his crops, and make his weapon. . . . Your daughters will be forced to make perfumes for him and work as his cooks and his bakers. He will take your best fields, vineyards, and olive groves, and give them to his officials. . . . He will take your servants and your best cattle. . . . And you yourselves will become his slaves.*
> *(1 Sam. 8:10–17)*

Millennia before Thomas Jefferson, the Israelites refused God's warning against kingly power. It was as true in 1776 BC as in AD 1776 that men who see themselves as born to reign, or born to steal the reins, are already corrupt or soon corrupted by power. Crumbs and oppression are the dividends of such rule. While Christianity tolerated oppressive conduct, the world today is no place for any leader whose imagined glory robs the people of their divine rights. No unelected man has the right to govern another. Any man, when asked to rule, does so as the servant of the people who chose him for a limited time and is subject to scrutiny and criticism.

Colonial America and colonial Judea both suffered under despotic rule, but the Israelites more so. In ancient Jerusalem, Pontius Pilate exercised more local power as Caesar's representative than King George was ever able to exert over the Americans. Nevertheless, Jesus was under the impression that Caesar was entitled to the efforts, crops, and money of the Israelites. He taught:

> *Render therefore to Caesar the things that are Caesar's.*

This instruction is noted often but rarely questioned. Jesus' remark, however, is an affirmation of tyrannical colonialism. After all, what actually belonged to Caesar? He was a Roman emperor whose armies conquered and then took what they pleased. In the ancient Near East, that which belonged to Caesar was only power; and that which his governor rendered unto Jesus was death.

History shows that Jesus was no Jefferson when it came to making the case for liberty.

In fairness, however, the Bible and Jesus are locked in the time warp of lost millennia. Jesus was born in an occupied nation and never knew otherwise. He sought to liberate his people by securing their salvation, not their individual and collective autonomy on earth. In those days, Paul wrote and Christianity accepted that

> *everyone must obey state authorities, because no authority exists without God's permission, and God has put the existing authorities there. Whoever opposes the existing authority opposes what God has ordered; and anyone who does so will bring judgment on himself. (Rom. 13:1–2)*

In 1776, the British colonies were no longer willing to obey the authorities, and they certainly rejected apostle Paul's idea that King George ruled them with God's permission. It was time for decision. After a year of conflict and a decade of unavailing protest, Jefferson and other radicals in the Continental Congress convened in Philadelphia to consider the impossible: independence from the strongest nation on earth. A committee of five, which included Benjamin Franklin and Samuel Adams, was appointed to draft a declaration. Its chairman was Thomas Jefferson.

Jesus and Jefferson were both revolutionaries. At age thirty-three, Jesus took up the radical cause of massive religious reform in order to overthrow senseless ritual, rigid laws, and a culture of oppressive theology. At age thirty-three, Jefferson took up the cause of liberty to overthrow the oppressive monarchy by authoring the Declaration of Independence. What Jesus said became scripture and changed the world. What Jefferson wrote should become scripture, for it too has changed the world.

Seventeen hundred years separate the two revolutionaries, time enough for a benevolent God to have determined that a new world requires a new scripture.

Jesus had taught pacifism in the face of Roman colonialism:

> *If anyone slaps you on the right cheek, let him slap your left cheek too. . . . If one of the occupation troops forces you to carry his pack one mile, carry it two miles. (Matt. 5:39–41)*

Doctrines of pacifism and obedience adopted nearly two thousand years ago by a weak religious sect threatened with extinction were not the answer in 1776. God surely withdrew these New Testament teachings in Independence Hall, Philadelphia, and inspired something new and powerful. His answer to Jesus and Paul was the Declaration of Independence:

> *We hold these truths to be self-evident, that all men are created equal, that they are endowed by their Creator with certain unalienable Rights, that among these are Life, Liberty and the pursuit of Happiness. . . . That whenever any Form of Government becomes destructive of these ends, it is the Right of the People to alter or abolish it.*

Did God inspire Thomas Jefferson to pen these words? Reason suggests a divine hand at work. Either the Founding Fathers grievously sinned by disobeying Christian scripture, or God's view of the world had changed dramatically by 1776. Either the pacifism of early Christians was still God's way, or in liberty's cause the resorting to arms by George Washington and the colonials was the new way. Which was the divine lesson?

Washington, Jefferson, and their colleagues fit the measure of divine intervention. What they sought to do—and then accomplished—was absolutely new in history. No group of men has done anything equal since. They nobly declared independence, won a war against the world's great military power, and then constructed a novel form of government to secure their liberties. After fighting and dying for their cause, they gave the world *government of the people, for the people, and by the people.*

The accomplishment of the Founding Fathers was not to predict the end of the world—the final verdict of old scripture—but to construct a new one. For the first time in history, individuals would have ownership of their rights, their government, and their ability to pursue happiness. This was not perfectly accomplished, but its perfection shines brilliantly in comparison to all that had preceded it from the beginning of time. A large republic was to be owned by its citizen stakeholders; its leaders were of their choosing for temporary periods to secure their liberties. This radical notion is today largely taken for granted. Legatees tend to feel that way. However, when seriously looking at the revolutionary scope of this eighteenth-century accomplishment, it is miraculous.

Jefferson's incredible contribution to the progress of mankind was written on a portable desk of his own design in a room he rented from a Philadelphia bricklayer. Congress adopted the resulting Declaration of Independence, with few changes on July 4, 1776, in Independence Hall, Philadelphia. There were twin results: a new nation was born, and a new purpose for having one:

> *That to secure these rights [of Life, liberty, and the pursuit of Happiness], Governments are instituted among Men, deriving their just powers from the consent of the governed . . . laying its foundation on such principles . . . as to them shall seem most likely to effect their Safety and Happiness.*

What would Pharaoh, Caesar, Attila, Hitler, Stalin, or Fidel Castro say to such a declaration of individual liberty? Did they hold office as *elected servants* of the governed to secure the people's inalienable rights? No such thing existed before, even back to the Garden of Eden. The Founding Fathers turned the world upside down. The divine right of the king was replaced by the divine right of liberty. The apostle Paul had overturned the Mosaic Code, and then wrote that obedience to civil authorities was divine law. Jefferson overturned King George's rule, and then wrote that disobedience to evil authorities was divine law. Upon which man was the light of providence shining?

The Declaration of Independence is a magnificent tablet. It deserves to be cherished by its beneficiaries—all mankind—as part of a new covenant, the Final Testament. The energizing influence of America's birth certificate remains vibrant, and its principles still remain the best weapon in the fight against mass evil.

The Declaration was addressed not only to Great Britain, from which independence was declared, but also to "the tribunal of the world." It was a remarkable call for a universal hearing of the case for freedom against tyranny. That was unique. One may ask, "Why not just meet, make the decision for revolution, and then resort to arms?" Answered Jefferson:

> *This was the object of the Declaration of Independence . . . to place before mankind the common sense of the subject, in terms so plain and firm as to command their assent, and to justify ourselves in the independent stand we are compelled to take.*

How bold to place before mankind that all men are created equal when nowhere in the world was that view more than a blasphemy. Elsewhere, men were neither free nor equal, not even imperfectly so in the ways Jefferson wrote. So, ringing the bell of liberty across the oceans was not really a call for approval by other free men since none had the freedoms for which the colonials chose to fight, but a call for the disapproval of despotism. These courageous men going to war for freedom did so "with a firm reliance on the protection of divine providence."

Although the revolutionaries had justified their revolution to the world, only God's blessing was needed. The birth of this revolution would not be in a manger hidden away from a wicked king. Quite the contrary, the birth of this new nation was in Philadelphia, the English-speaking world's second-largest city; and its delivery declared to the wicked king and all mankind. There was no fearful fleeing in the middle of the night. The nation was born in the light of a new day, July 4, 1776.

Jefferson's love of the cleansing tool of revolution was profound and enduring. Long after 1776 and his years of service as ambassador, secretary of state, vice president, president, and elder statesmen, he argued powerfully for continuing rebellion against man's devouring instincts:

> *If once they become inattentive to the public affairs . . . Congress . . . judges, and governors shall all become wolves. It seems to be the law of our general nature, in spite of individual exceptions; and experience declares than man is the only animal which devours its own kind, for I can apply no milder term to the governments of Europe, and to the general prey of the rich on the poor. I hold it that a little rebellion now and then is a good thing, and as necessary in the political world as storms in the physical. . . . It is a medicine necessary for the sound health of government.*

Indeed, Jefferson remained so attuned to the general nature of mankind to prey upon each other, he suggested that every generation ought to have its house-cleaning rebellion:

> *God forbid we should ever be twenty years without such a rebellion. . . . If they remain quiet such . . . lethargy [is] the forerunner of death to the public liberty. . . . The tree of liberty must be refreshed from time to time with the blood of patriots and tyrants. It is its natural manure.*

Thomas Jefferson continued his remarkable writings even from his deathbed. His love of liberty and his parallel distaste for what he believed were the New Testament's chains of ignorance were as clear as ever on June 24, 1826, when he wrote regarding the upcoming fiftieth anniversary of the Declaration of Independence. Jefferson's words stir our hearts:

> *May it be to the world what I believe [American indepen-dence] will be (to some parts sooner, to others later, but finally to all), the signal of arousing men to burst the chains under which monkish ignorance and superstition had persuaded them to bind themselves, and to assume the blessings and security of self-government . . . All eyes are opened, or are opening, to the rights of man. The general spread of the light of science has already laid open to every view the palpable truth that the mass of mankind has not been born with saddles on their backs, nor a favored few booted and spurred, ready to ride them legitimately by the grace of God . . . For ourselves let the annual return of this day [July 4] forever refresh our recollec-tions of these rights, and an undiminished devotion to them.*

Ten days later, while displays of fireworks burst across America in celebration of fifty years of independence, Thomas Jefferson died. Was he God's instrument for good? Are the "unalienable rights" of the Declaration of Independence inalienable only because revolutionaries said so, or because, like the heart and mind, they dwell within man at God's insistence?

Chapter Twenty-two

Constitution of the United States

The world's oldest national constitution was completed in Philadelphia by a convention presided over by George Washington, from May 1787 until September 17, 1787. It begins:

> *We the people of the United States, in order to form a more perfect Union, establish justice, insure domestic tranquility, provide for the common defense, promote the general welfare, and secure the blessings of liberty to ourselves and to our posterity, do ordain and establish this Constitution for the United States of America.*

Its primary author was the Virginian, James Madison. It is a thoroughly unique charter specifically intended to overcome the inherently evil thoughts of man. In that sense, it set out to do in America what no other people had ever accomplished. That would require a miracle. The hand of providence is visible in the two centuries of freedom that the Constitution has secured for Americans, and by example, to more than two billion others.

The Bible and the Constitution have a common purpose: a response to evil. The Old Testament failed in its purpose, and therefore ended with an apocalyptic call for a fresh start. The New Testament then arrived. It recognized again that evil was winning over goodness and, thus, provided for salvation in heaven rather than on earth. With there being little further use for earth, Christians ended their scripture with news of a coming apocalypse. Some 1,500 years later, James Madison took a revolutionary approach to the eternal problem of mass evil, and history has proven the Constitution he authored to be more effective than prior scriptural remedies.

James Madison was born March 31, 1751, in Orange County, Virginia. The Madison family had long been landowners in the colony, and James grew up on his father's plantation along the Rappahannock River. Providence seems to have blessed Virginia with an unusual number of exceptional leaders, including Thomas Jefferson, George Washington, Patrick Henry, and Madison, among many.

Following graduation from college in Princeton, New Jersey, Madison returned to Virginia where he was drawn to public affairs. King George's bent toward tyranny stirred the revolutionary pot, and Madison became immersed in Virginia's revolutionary atmosphere. In 1776, while only twenty-five, he served as a delegate to the Virginia convention to consider secession from Britain. Soon thereafter, Madison and Thomas Jefferson coauthored the first state constitution for Virginia. Their colleague Patrick Henry had uttered the famous words, "Give me liberty or give me death," and the answer was liberty.

Following the Declaration of Independence on July 4, 1776, General George Washington took charge of the troops who were to fight the war for independence from Great Britain. Much has been written of the military mismatch: untrained and ill-equipped American irregulars against the world's most effective fighting force. By all measures, England should have won. Had the king prevailed against the rebels, we would not have our Constitution. However, the highly improbable did occur, and the mostly ragtag Americans defeated the British in 1781.

Recall that God had given the Hebrews the gift of the Promised Land, but even after fighting for 250 gruesome years their victory was only partial. By contrast, fighting for the promise of their land, the American colonials achieved total victory in five years.

Success in war, however, did not bring immediate success in peace. Following their victory, the thirteen newly freed states were joined together under the Articles of Confederation, a loose political union that demonstrated a sorry fact in human affairs: where selfishness has sway, it will undermine good intentions. Thus, the Articles were an abysmal failure, prompting the Founding Fathers to search for something better with which to bind their collective fates.

As interest grew in a new form of union, James Madison immersed himself in all available studies of prior confederations: Greek city-states, Medieval Italian cities, the Holy Roman Empire, the German states, and others. In each case, jealousies and animosities brought every union to disaster. History taught that all prior efforts at republican government had failed because the majority trampled the rights of the minority, the strong rode over the weak, and the selfish ignored the group's general welfare. Such were the lessons James Madison took to heart in 1786.

How then to construct a defense against evil? That was the task in the face of another ugly historical truth noted in *The Federalist* by Madison—that men are not to be trusted with power because they are:

> *selfish, passionate, and full of whims, caprices, and preju-dices. . . . Moreover, the nature of man is a constant; it has had these characteristics throughout recorded history.*

And, as revealed in the Bible, the same characteristics dominated during prerecorded history as well.

Eleven years after the signing of the Declaration of Independence, the Constitutional Convention began in May 1787, in the very same Independence Hall in Philadelphia. At age eighty-one, wise old Benjamin Franklin attended every session. Former commander-in-chief George Washington presided. Once again, a remarkable and extraordinarily gifted group of men assembled to change the course of history. All were intent on finding a path to a republican union in which liberty and prosperity could thrive. Madison later said of his fellow delegates:

> *individually and collectively . . . there never was an assem-bly of men, charged with a great and arduous trust, who were*

more pure in their motives, or more exclusive or anxiously devoted to the object committed to them.

The stakes in the constitutional debate were high. History repeats itself because man's nature repeats itself. The issue in 1787 was whether America would repeat Europe's tragedies. It was feared that the convention's failure might lead to thirteen feuding states or perhaps to three or four hostile groupings. There was much to fight about: territory, commercial rivalries, maritime competition, western expansion, Indian problems, border insecurities, mineral rights, and religious issues, among many other flash points. The Americans knew that European nations were never at a loss for quarrels or wars. They also knew that the disposition toward conflict knows no boundaries; human nature in Boston or Charleston is no different than in Florence or Vienna.

Thus, a warring American continent was a possibility, and anyone familiar with the Bible's history of the twelve Hebrew tribes would have been justly concerned for the thirteen American states.

Madison was assigned the task of writing a constitution, and he was intent on finding a new formula for success. In mingling with the delegates, the erudite Virginian heard seemingly irreconcilable complaints. However, Madison's knowledge of the failed terrain of two thousand years of republican government won converts to his revolutionary approach.

Through argument and debate, discussion and dinner conversation, James Madison's formula for a new government began to take hold. His draft of the Constitution was accepted with only minor changes, and one important understanding regarding a Bill of Rights. Madison's draft did not include such a bill—the Constitution's famous first ten amendments—because of complicated political considerations tied to states' rights. However, convention delegates agreed that amendments specifying inalienable personal liberties would be added as part of the approval process. True to their agreement, it came to pass in 1791 as the Bill of Rights: the first ten amendments to the Constitution.

The general principles of the Constitution of the United States are reasonably well known. Although they may even be accepted as commonplace today, the new charter for liberty developed in 1787 was revolutionary. Freedom was fighting evil in a new way, and a changed history has been the result. The key principles are:

1. A strong and independent president with sufficient power to lead
2. A legislature consisting of two chambers based upon different representations and for different terms of years
3. An independent judiciary with ultimate authority over constitutional interpretation
4. Each branch has the constitutional means and personal motives to resist the others' encroachments
5. A Bill of Rights specifying broad personal liberties, which are inalienable
6. Provision for amending the Constitution by a large majority of the people.

The experiment in modern federalism begun in Philadelphia hinged on separation of powers between the three branches of government forced to coexist and function among meaningful checks and balances. The security of the people from the oppression of their government depends upon multiple safeguards. While it may appear as if the business of government would be stymied, the goal was for the business of evil to be stymied. The result has been the world's freest people operating a successful government with little modification since it began.

If there is to be a world in which the Creator's gift of unalienable rights becomes universal, there would need to be a constitutional starting point. That occurred in Philadelphia in 1787.

God's first constitution, ordained in the Sinai Desert, strictly controlled all aspects of the conduct of ordinary people. Individuals had to obey the Sabbath and were prohibited from committing adultery. A person could legally eat locusts but not move a neighbor's property line. On and on it went with great specificity:

If you have a dreaded skin disease, you must wear torn clothes, leave your hair uncombed, cover the lower part of your face, and call out, "Unclean, unclean!" (Lev. 13:45)

The people of Israel must no longer be unfaithful to the Lord by killing their animals in the fields as sacrifices to the goat demons. (Lev. 17:7)

After sexual intercourse both the man and the woman must take a bath, and they remain unclean until evening. (Lev. 15:18)

Nowhere, however, were there any restraints upon those who ruled—whether God or king. Such was the Lord's constitution. Three thousand years later, James Madison and his colleagues saw the world in reverse. Mass evil was coming from the very few having unrestrained power over the many. Thus, the architecture of a restrained government was a series of checks and balances upon the executive, the legislature, and the judiciary. Power centers would check and restrain each other, and in the Bill of Rights, personal rights were made inviolate, for example:

Amendment I: Congress shall make no law respecting an establishment of religion . . . or abridging the freedom of speech, or of the press; or the right of the people peaceably to assemble, and to petition the Government for a redress of grievances.

Amendment V: No person shall be . . . subject for the same offense to be twice put in jeopardy of life or limb; nor shall be compelled in any criminal case to be a witness against himself, nor be deprived of life, liberty, or property, without due process of law.

Checking power is the essence of the constitutional effort to rein in evil. No such restraints exist in the many places still ruled by tyrants, totalitarians, and thugs. When inalienable rights like those contained in the Bill of Rights are stolen, their owners truly suffer, and the rest of the world is imperiled.

Of course, the eighteenth-century revolution was not perfect. An open discussion of the constitution's guarantee of liberty must face the criticism that the thirteen colonies' half million slaves labored on untouched by its freedoms. For the black people doing much backbreaking work, there were no inalienable rights, and certainly there were tyrannical slave masters among the many owners. We may ask, "Why was there no divine inspiration for the most oppressed?"

Slavery has existed from the beginning of time. Even God's favorite, the patriarch Abraham owned slaves. After the Hebrews were rescued from 420 years of slavery in Egypt, they enslaved others during the march across Sinai. Two of the Ten Commandments acknowledged the practice:

> *Observe the Sabbath and keep it holy. . . . On that day no one is to work—neither you, your children, your **slaves**, your animals, nor the foreigners who live in your country. (Exod. 20:8–10; emphasis added))*

> *Do not desire another man's house; do not desire his wife, his **slaves**, his cattle, his donkeys, or anything else that he owns. (Exod. 20:9–10, 17; emphasis added)*

Many other sections of the Mosaic Code regulate the practice of slavery, as we have already seen, including the circumcision of slaves attending the Passover dinner.

Later, the New Testament contained the Christian message that slaves should work hard and be faithful. Thus, apostle Paul urged:

> *Slaves, obey your earthly masters with deep respect and fear. Serve them sincerely as you would serve Christ. (Eph. 6:5)*

In 1775, Thomas Jefferson introduced legislation in Virginia that would have given the colony's slave owners the option of freeing their human chattel. King George said no. Later, in 1787, the issue was much discussed during the Constitutional Convention. Many were ready to abolish the practice. Virtually all the delegates acknowledged the immorality of human ownership. Nevertheless, in the end, the Founding Fathers and the spirit that animated them determined that the end of slavery in America must await another day.

However imperfect it was, republican democracy creatively devised was by itself a revolutionary leap forward. God and Madison could achieve no more in 1787. Freedom was not complete, but it became so later, and many who died in its cause were buried in Gettysburg, Pennsylvania. There, President Abraham Lincoln stated, in 1863:

> *[T]his nation under God, shall have a new birth of freedom—and that the government of the people, by the people, for the people, shall not perish from the earth.*

The first sentence of the Bible states, "In the beginning, when God created the universe, the earth was formless and desolate." Much has happened on earth since. Recall that in the Bible's first look at government, Egypt was a nation ruled by a series of god-kings exercising absolute power. Thus, Pharaoh had the power to order death for all Hebrew firstborn or freedom for all Hebrews whenever born. Millions of ordinary Egyptians suffered terribly because Pharaoh alone was empowered to say "stay" or "go" regarding the Hebrews. What individual rights did Egyptians have to prevent their own government from causing incalculable misery? Obviously, none.

Pharaoh was not concerned about running for reelection, but suppose reelection had been a worry, and he knew the electorate was grieving in the wake of his policy regarding Hebrew slavery. The answer to defeating mass evil in Pharaoh's Egypt is no different than the answer to ending oppression today. It has never been set forth with briefer eloquence than by Abraham Lincoln:

> *Government of the people, by the people, for the people.*

Slavery ended in the United States because a nation "conceived in liberty, and dedicated to the proposition that all men are created equal" (Lincoln) had the courage to innovate. That is the divine spirit of the Constitution of the United States, the second of the three documents offered as scripture in the Final Testament.

Chapter Twenty-three

The Federalist

The third book in the scripture of the Final Testament is *The Federalist*. This work consists of eighty-five essays published in New York newspapers during 1787–1788 in support of adoption of the pending Constitution of the United States. Appearing under the pen name Publius, the authors were James Madison, Alexander Hamilton, and John Jay. Madison, of course, was the brilliant draftsman of the Constitution. Hamilton was a New Yorker of Jamaican birth, whose powerful mind added greatly to the success of the American experiment. Later, he became secretary of the Treasury under President Washington, whom he had served as advisor during the War for Independence. Hamilton was a man of great intellectual heft.

The third contributor to Publius was John Jay. He was a successful New York lawyer, a delegate to the Constitutional convention, political pragmatist, and a key figure in the vigorous effort necessary to win adoption of the Constitution by the states.

These three men writing together as Publius but often working independently co-authored the definitive work on representative republican government. The Constitution was a radical departure from all prior efforts to govern unions of people, and Publius' role was to demonstrate how and why the evil in man's nature had been effectively targeted. The Federalist Papers argued convincingly that the new architecture of liberty would endure against the stresses of human nature.

The long process of public debate began immediately after September 17, 1787, when the Constitutional Convention in Philadelphia adjourned. Should the Constitution be adopted? Conventions were convened in every state to argue its merits. The intense debate lasted for ten months, but the foremost arguments were by

Publius. Although the essays were addressed "To the People of the State of New York," where they appeared in newspapers, they were widely circulated throughout the states. The essays were then bound in book form in 1788 for additional distribution and impact.

The Federalist Papers was written for a specific purpose in a unique historic moment. In its day, it played the role of the Sunday morning talk shows, with intelligent discourse on the most important issue before the nation. However, it is better and smarter than that. It speaks to all men everywhere, in all generations about the philosophy and mechanics of governance. Publius looked at history's large canvas and saw that during the prior two thousand years, virulent tyranny had brought down all previous republican governments. Prior to 1787, the checking and balancing of man's instincts for evil had been imperfectly constructed or nonexistent. With such a sorry set of precedents, James Madison and his colleagues could never be certain if their constitutional framework would withstand natural selfishness.

What had Madison, Hamilton, and Jay seen in the historic precedents?

> *The history of almost all the great councils and consultations held among mankind for reconciling their discordant opinions . . . may be classed among the most dark and degraded pictures which display the infirmities and depravities of the human character. (Federalist 27–28)*

To modern ears, this may be quaint language, but the point is clear. *The Federalist* is warning of "the caprice and wickedness of man" (Federalist 28), or more politely stated:

> *Antagonistic and immediate interests have greater efficacy than true interests and motives of reason and virtue.*

Importantly, Publius made clear to its readers that America was not an historic exception to the worst in human nature. The newly freed states had no

> *exemption from the imperfections, weaknesses, and evils incident to society in every shape. (Federalist 6)*

This recognition that human nature in America is like that in the rest of the world is an extraordinary point. In colonial America, the perception existed that the New World was different because it was far from the diseased heart of Europe. Imbued with a strong taste for liberty, the modest colonies had defeated a powerful king to throw off unjust bindings. So was the American heart in 1787 uninfected with the "evil thoughts" God recognized in people from "the time they are young"? If so, no constitution would have been needed.

It would have been folly for American revolutionaries to imagine their new status heralded a reformed heart. In his autobiography, God had once promised a change of human heart, but that project was abandoned. Thus, the Constitution was programmed to deal with unreformed hearts. Madison's pen reflected the universal truth about human nature and avoided the popular fiction that evil was dead in America.

Two centuries have borne witness to the positive effects worldwide of the acceptance of individual liberties. There is everywhere among people a human energy capable of great things when divine freedoms are exercised in the pursuit of dreams. Everywhere energetic freedoms exist, there is protection against arbitrary power. There is no rich or successful nation run by a dictator, nor can there be. With freedom, people flower, innovate, do big things, and the planet is enriched. Free nations prosper. Dictatorships produce misery.

Only two centuries old, divine liberty is a young miracle of good against evil, without biblical peer. The revolution of constitutional success has been the engine powering an unparalleled wave of freedom all across the world. Whereas Christ's ascension was an unrecorded secret affair for the very few, the Constitution's ascension in the sight of all has been a celebration for the very many.

Which rising was favored by God's hand?

Chapter Twenty-four

The Necessity of Virtue

T he American Reformation was delivered by the Founding Fathers with a warning: its principles supporting liberty will not endure without a healthy diet of virtue. As John Adams wrote:

> *Liberty can no more exist without virtue and independence than a body can live and move without a soul.*

Some contemporary sophisticates may suggest that religious discussion of honesty, responsibility, respect, and duty is unbearably quaint, or that the postmodern world will carry on nicely without lectures on compassion, self-discipline, and courage. However, they might recall the words of the worldly-wise young French nobleman, Alexis de Tocqueville. He was by far the most perceptive foreign observer of early America. His voice added elegantly to the importance of virtue:

> *I sought for the greatness and genius of America in her commodious harbors and her ample rivers, and it was not there; in her fertile fields and boundless prairies; and it was not there; in her rich mines and her vast commerce, and it was not there. . . . America is great because she is good, and if America ever ceases to be good, America will cease to be great.*

George Washington said it more to the point:

> *Human rights can only be assured among a virtuous people. The general government . . . can never be in danger of degenerating into a monarchy, an oligarchy, an aristocracy, or any despotic or oppressive form so long as there is any virtue in the body of people.*

The Final Testament's reformed scripture would be accompanied by the study of virtue because it is the mortar holding together liberty's foundations. We are either virtuous and tend to our community of needs, or over time the fabric of liberty will wear thin, fray, and return to biblical chaos. We ought to be virtuous not because our grandparents told us we should be, but because without it our grandchildren may tell of liberty lost:

> *A vitiated state of morals, a corrupted public conscience, is incompatible with freedom. No free government, or the blessings of liberty, can be preserved to any people but by a firm adherence to justice, moderation, temperance, frugality, and virtue; and by a frequent recurrence to fundamental principles. (Patrick Henry)*

We should not be shy or embarrassed about virtue. It is not a cliché, but a need. It is not just for rural folks but also for the smart, the hip, the young, and the middle-aged. Without virtue, we slowly lose what we have, and that is hardly trendy. The American Reformation's liberty will not exist in a moral vacuum. It needs good people or people at least trying to be good. Moreover, city sophisticates in the pursuit of happiness might experiment with virtue:

> *Good acts give us pleasure . . . because nature hath implanted in our breasts a love of others, a sense of duty to them, a moral instinct, in short which prompts us irresistibly to feel and succor their distresses. (Thomas Jefferson)*

The world's evil doesn't tire. It is always ready for a fight; and Final Testament congregations can emphasize without embarrassment that it is good to be responsible, generous, and compassionate and to show mercy, humility, and love. Not because virtue is a ticket to heaven or a moral fashion statement, but because it is the ground floor of freedom, holding up the rest of the structure.

Pope John Paul II spoke and wrote often regarding the truth that freedom untethered from morality risks self-destruction. He wisely observed that a vibrant moral culture is essential for democracy, for only such a culture can affirm the virtues necessary to assure liberty's health. In this regard, the venerated pope echoed the Founding Fathers whose inspired wisdom taught that merely getting the institutions right is not enough; freedom's future depends on society's knowing and choosing the genuinely good.

Chapter Twenty-five

The Case for Faith by Faith

An omnipotent God could have designed history so that virtue was the natural force governing all. What an unimaginably different planet it would be as people lived their lives free from evil. Police and armies would be unnecessary. Indeed, government would probably be superfluous since all contact between people would be an exchange of goodness in one form or another. However fascinating such musings may be, God chose to have an earth bursting with wrongdoing, and we must deal with the consequences.

This portion of the book addresses the potentially different perspectives among the faiths in their consideration of new scripture. In one sense it is an error to suggest that Christianity, Judaism, and Islam may have separate reasons for adopting the Final Testament since all three cheer good works and decry evil. There is a common humanity before a tag for this faith or that is pinned to our identities. Yet life's experience shows that three brothers going their separate ways, even if calling home to the same father, will over time develop different realities, sacred and otherwise. Thus, while a new scripture emphasizing dynamic liberty offers universal benefits, real-life differences should be acknowledged.

Judaism

For modern Jews, the path to canonization of America's founding documents is the road to the Promised Land. Judaism should experience no bumps in embracing revolutionary freedoms as holy writ.

Since Assyria conquered northern Israel in 721 BC and exiled its people, the ancient Jewish tribes have been almost continually subjugated and dispersed. After the Assyrians came the Egyptians, the Babylonians, the Persians, the Greeks, and the Romans. All this even before Jesus was born. Then it became worse as persecutions inflicted endless suffering through the ages.

The biblical census taken during the exodus from Egypt counts six hundred thousand adult males. Were there perhaps two million Hebrews then? We cannot know the full number with any certainty. Today, more than three thousand years later, the number is only perhaps fourteen million. By today's global standards, this is a very small group. The Old Testament concept of chosenness—being God's special people, or as the Bible often says, "his beloved slaves"—has not protected the Jews from the most horrific suffering at the hands of God and the godless. Most recently, the Holocaust of World War II claimed the Jews for unspeakable horrors. Now, five million Jews live in danger in Israel, an armed camp the size of New Jersey, under threat from far more numerous and larger neighbors unburdened by the restraints of democracy.

The United States is the true Promised Land for the world's Jews, among many other groups, because here they have found more freedom, security, and prosperity than ever before in history, whether under Moses, Solomon, Rabbi Jesus, or anyone since. In 1790, General George Washington visited the Jewish synagogue in Newport, Rhode Island, and committed to that congregation that America would forever honor its commitment to religious freedom for all. It has. Whatever Jews may have hoped to achieve in the biblical Promised Land, they have realized in America.

In thankful response to America's liberties and the unparalleled personal security the country provides, Jews in the United States have become staunch advocates of personal freedom. As a group, it has the nation's highest percentage of voters. Through political, legal, and financial efforts, Jews have raised a powerful collective voice that openly cherishes our Constitution. It would be difficult to identify another group in the United States that equals America's Jewish citizenry in commitment to the constitutional processes. In practice, then, the descendants of the Old Testament tribes are already faithful to the Final Testament.

Judaism blossomed into a full faith when on Mount Sinai God presented the Jewish Law to Moses and the newly freed Hebrews. The 613 statutes were tailored for tribes trekking in the desert on their way to nationhood. They were an ancient people in a distant land, with cultural needs far removed from our modern understanding. In response to concern about the evil of adultery, the Lord decreed that adulterers be killed; homosexuals, the same; disrespectful children, the same. The law represented an intertwining of religious, criminal, and social considerations in a superstitious world ruled by priests serving as God's administrators. However, that is no longer our world.

Because we inhabit a different world, a large majority of Jews today mostly reject or ignore Judaism, the religion. By contrast, they cling to Judaism, the culture. Thus, modern Jews may or may not believe in the living God of the Bible, but they do believe that life is lived in this world rather than the next, and everyone should be as good, fair, and loving as possible. That is largely the sum of Jewish religious belief for the majority of America's Jews. To that, the faith's deep cultural traditions add much richness to the mostly secular experience.

Contemporary Judaism's extraordinary commitment to the values of liberty comes not from the Bible's Mosaic code, but rather in response to millennia of hideous persecution and involuntary dispersion. The Jewish people are thankful beneficiaries of the Constitution. Recognizing the miraculous, one may ask, "If the God of Moses handed down 613 statutes to govern twelve tribes, why not a Constitution to govern thirteen states"? The leap of faith is not great. What an amazingly uplifting revelation that George Washington, Thomas Jefferson, James Madison, and other Protestant revolutionaries were inspired by the God of Moses to deliver a new law, bringing liberty to America and by example to the world.

Today, at 2,500 years old, the Hebrew Bible still ends with the promise of apocalypse because evil was more rampant than the Lord could stomach. This reflects another truth: that the Old Testament God was mostly jealous, vindictive, murderous, and often nearly crazed with wrath. Of course, those prone to seeing goodness in all things would answer that God was acting out of love and justice: that he loved his people, demanded their devotion to justice—as defined in severe tribal code—and then protected or punished them as their conduct warranted.

However, the Bible's books speak eloquently for themselves, and all Jews, whether orthodox or merely by tradition, should summon the courage to recognize certain truths: the truth as to God's revealed personality; and the truth that nearly all Jews have virtually abandoned the *religion* of their long-gone ancestors. If doubt persists, then doubters should read again the books of Exodus, Deuteronomy, and Leviticus. Then they may ask themselves if the faith they practice resembles the faith of the fundamentalist tribal society that received the often surrealistic law. Substantively, the law is nearly gone.

Certainly, the acceptance of one God, Judaism's extraordinary bequest to Western society, is at the heart of the faith, but for millennia, there has been nothing unique in that. The very same God is the Lord to all Christians, the Allah of Islam, and the spiritual focus to untold additional millions of faithful who accept the Lord.

Jews should reflect carefully upon the state of their contemporary faith and see in the Final Testament the potential for an extraordinary renewal. The new scripture already exists passionately in the hearts and lives of the Jewish community. It needs only to be recognized formally as the divine will of a Lord now intent on arming all people with freedom and liberty in the war to end mass evil.

Then there is the important matter of Israel. God had promised Abraham that his seed would be as numerous as the sand in the sea, and the Promised Land would reach from the Nile to the Euphrates. Today, there are more Texans than Jews, and the stretch from Egypt to Iraq has never been the home of the chosen.

Indeed, from before Jesus until President Harry S. Truman, the Jews had no homeland, only 2,400 years of a broken covenant and stubborn faith. World Jewry today is a tiny minority among the earth's six billion people. Israel is a small nation struggling for neighborhood respect. Born in bloodshed, Israel has never known peace and is surrounded by much larger enemies seeking its destruction.

Nevertheless, modern Israel embraced the power of democratic liberties for its citizens and prospers despite constant mortal danger. The truth is, however, Israel survives against the enmity of its neighbors only because the United States is an energetic democracy still believing in its revolutionary ideals. It is protective of the robustly democratic Jewish state shaped by survivors of Hitler. America's miracle has been Israel's miracle too. Israel can recognize the three documents of the Final Testament as Holy Scriptures, part of an amended Torah. Judaism can honor as God's prophets Jefferson, Washington, Franklin, Adams, Madison, and Hamilton, men whose legacy of liberty has crossed oceans to an oppressed world. July 4 can be a national holiday in Israel. Moses need not suffer because Thomas Jefferson is celebrated as a prophet for writing that all men are created equal. The Founding Fathers of America are also founding fathers to democratic Israel, and may properly be honored as such.

Above all, there is this truth: what happened in the American colonies two hundred years ago was, beyond any shadow of a doubt, the greatest miracle to survival of the Jewish people in more than two thousand years. Let the Jewish faithful and Israel say it is so. Amen.

Christianity

This volume poses an agonizing question for many Christians: Was Jesus' birth and crucifixion the final divine act upon which peace hinges? And redemption for the earth's six billion? If so, then the world has done a poor job in recognizing it or bearing its evidence. Did the scriptures close with the New Testament? Is it really God's final word for all time to come, or did he deliver a new word for a new time through the hands and minds of the Founding Fathers and the American Reformation? The dilemma is a source of spiritual agony.

However, questioning key theology is a critical step in the process of change, especially momentous change. The bricks and mortar at the bottom of our belief system must shake before our hearts and minds can open toward the new and revolutionary. Understandably, whether Mary's was a virgin birth, or Jesus' ministry a prelude to a new and final covenant, are uncomfortable questions. Many of the faithful may respond, "Let it be. It was so long ago, and who can know what happened?" To that may be added, "Anyway, what difference does it make? Only Jesus' words matter, and tomorrow I will still be driving through rush hour to work no matter what." Fair comment on the road to revolution.

If nothing else, Jesus was a revolutionary. Judaism had been the religion of his tribe for a thousand years. He was born and circumcised in that tradition and at age twelve impressed the rabbis with his remarkable Hebrew knowledge. However, the Jewish experience to Jesus' time had largely been an historical failure. The Hebrew Bible was well-known to Jesus—he often cited its passages—and its history showed his people falling victim to foreign sword or slavery even while held hostage to God's rigid laws. A daily reminder of the national tragedy was that Jesus spoke Aramaic, the tongue the Israelites adopted during their Babylonian enslavement. That sorry episode was part of a Mediterranean Diaspora in response to endless warfare, punishment by God, and persecution. Meanwhile, those like Jesus who remained in the Promised Land lived with little promise under heavy Roman rule.

Being a revolutionary is no easy matter. It requires courage far beyond the modest calls needed for life's daily battles. The ultimate sacrifice of life may be part of the bargain. In the Roman milieu, in the Jewish tradition, and in the daily struggle for survival in a poor land, Jesus showed remarkable courage as he sought remarkable change. Regrettably, however, Jesus didn't live long enough to develop fully his revolutionary theories. Eighteen months of ministry is insufficient time to formulate a response to 613 laws and develop alternative traditions.

Jesus was also part of the apocalyptic tradition. Hebrew prophecy had long said that God's displeasure with his earthly experiment was so great that destruction was the only answer. How sorry a verdict that was. How unhappy must have been Jesus' vision of omnipresent evil, evil that was everywhere and present in everyone. Why else must the verdict be the end of the world? Any milder vision could have been resolved with a milder sentence. If the earth was worth saving, why not save it?

Thankfully, Jesus was wrong. The world did not end. However, many Christians today believe that Jesus' apocalyptic vision was correct, but only delayed. However, doesn't reason impose a statute of limitations on prophecies? Jesus spoke of God's expected cleaving of the earth nearly two thousand years ago. Before him, Isaiah gave a similar message nearly 2,800 years ago. Is it not fair to suggest that, given enough time, almost anything will come true? Jesus' words implied an imminent destruction, while the apostle Paul even cautioned against married life because there was so little time remaining.

This book is a call to religious revolution just as Jesus' ministry was in his day. Why revolution? The Hebrew Bible was centuries old. It seemed not to be working. Much of the law made little sense, and Jesus preached for momentous change. Divine or not, end of the world or not, his message remains that even God's final word—the closed Hebrew Bible of his faith—needed radical change to meet the people's needs. Thus, Jesus said not to focus upon what went into one's mouth, as the ancient dietary laws required, but what came out of it. The "eternal" word needed revolutionary change.

Christianity was therefore born as a revolutionary faith. God, seemingly tired of the losing battle against evil conducted under the Mosaic code, changed direction in favor of salvation through faith. God was doing an about face. Believe in Jesus, and rewards will follow. No more rigid and burdensome Mosaic code, no more circumcision, and no more difficult dietary restrictions. Christianity was both a revolution of faith and a revolution of personal rights. Most of all, it was a new direction in promoting goodness and fighting evil. God was the revolutionary and Jesus his George Washington, the general leading the troops.

The need today for another reformation in faith is great. Jesus and Paul talked of God's cleaving the earth in two. Today, however, monumental disasters may have many creators, most of them malevolent. The opportunity for cataclysm is far greater as technical progress continues to render destruction easier.

Time has provided today's world a larger frame within which to picture history's events since Jesus. Some people believe God has been absent for the past two millennia. Others believe his hand has shaped many miracles, large and small. However, time's journal from the days of Roman torture stakes to the mixed blessings of today's world shows that the American Revelation for liberty has liberated more people from oppression than anything else. Christ and his disciples were God's army for change. Can we not have faith that God saw again the need for revolutionary change and carried it out through the American Revelation?

Should American colonials have followed Jesus' teaching and offered two miles of pack portage to an occupying British soldier demanding only one mile? Who would have offered such a thing to a Nazi storm trooper? Only someone who truly believed the world was ending next month, and that kindness to an oppressor would assure a place in heaven. But God seems finally to have rejected that notion in 1776. Freedom's Declaration of Independence became the replacement for Christianity's declaration of dependence.

Of course, it goes without saying, that American Christians cheer the Revolutionary War and the liberty that resulted. Probably no one would agree with the pacifist notion that George Washington's troops should never have fired a bullet in anger. This truth only emphasizes the need to recognize a new scripture in which people have actual faith rather than frozen ritual. In this sense, the Final Testament celebrates the return of God after centuries of detachment to set the people right. Christianity virtuously calls out for each of us to "love thy neighbor." However, many people dislike their neighbors, and Robert Frost's observation, "Good fences make good neighbors," incorporates much human experience. Merely preaching an abstract form of goodwill has little practical effect upon evil in this world. If through faith we hope to diminish evil, then we should energize ourselves where mass efforts will really work. We must make sure that divine rights are universally inalienable through collective voices that governments cannot ignore.

Congregations of faith already exist everywhere, and everywhere they can send the message that a better life is possible. Pulpits can lead in proving Jefferson's words: "The God who gave us life gave us liberty at the same time."

The call by Christian congregations throughout the world to support universal personal liberty would be a divine mission against evil. Freedom should prevail wherever it remains a stranger. The tyrants, oppressors, bullies, thieves, and thugs who dictate over millions—whether in Cuba, Zaire, Syria, North Korea, Iran, Zimbabwe, Burma, or elsewhere—should be howled off stage. They should be hounded from office by an energized world voice—from within those countries and without—unwilling to tolerate any longer the alienation of "inalienable rights." If congregations raise their voices, the decent leaders of the world will hear and then follow. Until all people are free, the threat of mass evil remains.

In the cause of preserving life and liberty, Christians share the goal of teaching virtues. It is part of their tradition, and the Founding Fathers taught that virtue is a necessary ingredient for liberty. Therefore, teaching and doing right is more than civic duty; it is essential to preserve freedom. This carries on the Christian tradition of good works, which benefits equally those doing and those receiving.

Yet, another benefit would be the magnetism Final Testament Christian faith would have for young people, both as congregants and ministers. Bright and energetic men and women would be drawn to participate and lead. Today, a church calling is a "difficult sell" for too many young people because so much of Christian scripture is locked into a mysterious past. By contrast, religion moving to world peace based upon God's gift of revolutionary principles would be a powerful call to the best youth and the best that youth has to offer.

With a universal scripture, new church leaders can travel the world ministering to congregations hungry for what the Bill of Rights can bring to their lives. We can imagine a burst of constructive idealism as many of the best and brightest youth find a welcome home in the church and seek to spread the good news of inalienable rights and their sustaining virtues to needy communities in Africa, Asia, and Latin America. The regimes of despots, thugs, and callous manipulators would be the devils to slay. Such good work may be dangerous, but the miracle of people motivated for good is that they respond even in the face of danger. With intensely renewed purpose in religion's call for government of the people, by the people, and for the people, many young people—and others not so young—will accept the call.

The Bible tragically shows that evil doesn't tire. The last century showed that untiring evil is ever more violent and threatening. Therefore, Christianity can recall proudly that it was born nearly two thousand years ago with a revolutionary change in the battle plan in the fight for good against evil. Today is the right time to renew that revolution through a new divine covenant that, in the very changed world of today, may bring peace on earth.

Islam

The Final Testament is a gift to all. Yes, it was inspired in English rather than Arabic, but Muslims today speak Indonesian, Hindu, Malaysian, Persian, French, and dozens of other languages, including English. Allah, minding his universe, may find reason to speak through a Moroccan or a colonial Virginian. Always, we should be listening for the message. Moreover, the message today appears to be that Allah has ended the 1,400-year-old call for submission. One translation of "Islam" is *submission*; another is *peace*. Instead, there is the call for universal human rights, freedoms to speak, write, assemble, travel, vote, genuine due process, and the guarantee that elected leaders will support these freedoms. There is much about the future to consider, but first it is appropriate to visit the past.

In Islam, God's will was revealed in the Koran as received by Allah's messenger Muhammad during a twenty-year period beginning in about AD 610. At that time in history, the Jews were scattered throughout the lands of the Mediterranean, and Christian Europe had fallen into an epoch of darkness, decay, and death—the Dark Ages. Perhaps the Lord wanted light, and, therefore, sent his angels to deliver a new word to Muhammad, making him the last of God's messengers in the line that includes Adam, Noah, Abraham, Moses, Jesus, and others. Islam holds, therefore, that Allah wanted revolutionary change in the seventh century. That which went before was being replaced. The new word—the last word—had arrived.

Islam views man's purpose on earth as service and obedience to Allah. Such obedience will be imperfect, of course, because man is frail by nature and given to arrogance and pride. Thus, Allah knows that his imperfect followers will be susceptible to Satan's manipulations and, therefore, sometimes reject him. Yet, the merciful Allah is always ready to pardon. In this respect, Islam accepts the Adam and Eve story, including Adam's fall from grace, but Allah forgives Adam, thereby doing away with any concept of original sin.

The issue of evil is central to Islam because it observes a real and aggressive Satan who is always ready to do evil and often is successful. Such evil will cease only on the last day when the world will come to an end, and the dead will be resurrected. The good people will then go to a paradise containing many pleasures; the condemned will burn in hellfire. These doctrines, like much in the Bible, reflect the tribal views of their day because Allah's revelations do not step out of their time. They were born in the seventh century and declared to be unchangeable.

Unknown to many is that traditional Islam contains a powerful doctrine of social service directed toward alleviating suffering and helping the needy. The emphasis on service, part of the fight against evil, was able during early Islam to alleviate suffering among society's weakest members: women, orphans, the poor, and slaves. Indeed, emancipation of slaves was encouraged, and slaves were given rights, including the right to purchase their freedom. Also, distinction and privileges traditionally granted by tribal rank were abolished, and all men declared to be the equal children of Adam. Traditional Islam accords societal respect and rank through the recognition of good acts and piety. Here too the message of classic Islam needs to be broadcast better.

In its early dynamic phase, Islam burst from Arabia in the seventh century and within one hundred years had spread from India to Spain. For many centuries thereafter, the Islamic world was the seat of learning and culture while Christendom wallowed in the darkness of blind faith during an especially brutal epoch. At the time, an observer might have concluded that God favored a flowering Islam over a depressed Christianity and a dispersed Jewry.

However, the sun rises, and the sun sets.

Today, when we observe the Muslim world from Morocco on the Atlantic, across north Africa, through the Middle East to central Asia, and on to Indonesia in South Asia, we see, with few exceptions to a Muslim universe mostly mired in backwardness, impoverished, lacking in personal liberties, and home to oppressive governments.

Recently, the dimension of that failure was illustrated by the nation of Afghanistan during the Taliban period, which ended in 2001. Through perceived devotion to the Koran and God's prophet Muhammad, the theocratic Taliban enforced fundamentalist Islamic law, as they perceived it, with a biblical vengeance. Women had few rights and were required to remain covered. All symbols of foreign gods were destroyed. The tiny minority Hindu population was forced to wear identifying yellow patches. All education was from the Koran. Destruction for nonbelievers was a popular mantra. It was a dictatorship by the priests for Allah. Clergy dictated perceived holiness and in doing so imitated the worst in biblical life. The Taliban corrupted Islam and immeasurably harmed the perception of that religion in the minds of others.

Another leader disfiguring the face of Islam was Saddam Hussein. Unlike the theocratic Taliban, Hussein's regime was mostly secular, but totally ruthless. However, he managed to retain power in part because Islam has no contemporary voice in the sphere of human rights. The ancient roots of traditional Islam have been unreceptive to the idea of inalienable rights in the Western sense.

The result in Iraq was a tragedy. Saddam Hussein's blood-stained hands count perhaps one million dead by war, starvation, disease, or murder during his thirty years of dictatorship. Instead of securing people's liberties, the Hussein regime secured their poverty. Tragically, Allah rendered little assistance to the Iraqi people. Now a renewed Iraq struggles through the fire of terrorism to install democratic institutions that may finally allow the nation to prosper in freedom. However, opposing the birth of liberty is a horde of would-be tyrants and religious fundamentalists who kill and maim with Biblical/Koranic ferocity. Their beheadings leap from the pages of scripture. Ascribing no value to life or freedom, the terrorists in Iraq survive as tribal evildoers in a Near Eastern Jurassic Park of mayhem.

The story would have been dramatically otherwise if Islam's leaders recognized the Final Testament as new Islamic teaching, inspired by Allah, the one God. Prayers in the mosques in Iraq and throughout the Arab world would ask for help in securing voting rights, free speech, press, and assembly. People would be unaccepting of their oppression, and seek to vanquish their oppressors. This energy for a divine-rights movement would topple the dictators. They could no longer control the people wanting what Jefferson and Madison delivered for Allah. Hussein would have been gone years before his military defeat, booted out by empowered Iraqis demanding their Bill of Rights and an elected government.

Muslims would do well to experience the dynamism of these words:

> *We hold these truths to be self-evident, that all men are created equal, that they are endowed by their Creator with certain unalienable Rights, that among them are Life, Liberty, and the pursuit of Happiness. (Declaration of Independence)*

And these:

> *[The government] shall make no law . . . abridging the freedom of speech, or of the press; or the right of the people to peaceably assemble, and to petition the Government for a redress of grievances. (Cons. Amend. I)*

And these:

> *That whenever any Form of Government becomes destructive of [these unalienable rights], it is the right of the people to alter or abolish it, and to institute new Government . . . as to them shall seem most likely to effect their Safety and Happiness. (Declaration of Independence)*

These words are inspirational. In the Declaration of Independence, Jefferson's vision of the Creator's empowering hand generates an inner glow. They are words filled with potential and reward. This is a positive creed. It is a call to act upon life in this world, rather than in the next. It is a world in which government does not ration limited rights but exists to protect the people's inalienable rights. Dynamic and constructive change occurs when there is government of the people, by the people, and for the people.

It is for the Muslim people to find their own way. From Morocco to Indonesia, one billion faithful practice diverse strands of Islam in nations yielding few liberties or opportunities for fulfillment. Turkey is a bright exception as it embraces personal freedom, while Indonesia shows progress, and a liberated Iraq nurses early democratic hopes. Mostly, however, Muslims are poor and lead difficult lives. Intolerance sets high barriers to happiness and success. If honest, Asian and African Muslims would observe today that Allah's rewards on earth for their faith are few. The result must be partly due to Islam's demand for submission, which has the psychological effect of diminishing certain positive impulses. Thus, the instincts to wonder and create are made servile to faith, and the pursuit of happiness is subdued during the wait for Allah's kindness.

Under such circumstances, it is fair to ask, "Is Allah offering something more than we have seen or experienced?" How would anyone know for sure if a divine hand were at work? We could not know for sure. However, as a beginning point, it is suggested that Muslims expand their observations beyond their own backyard. Perhaps a miracle from Allah could occur in Australia or Peru. Perhaps a man, or even a woman, inspired by Allah would be speaking Russian, Bantu, Portuguese, or English. Perhaps his name would be Rodriguez, Goldberg, Hussani, or Polowski. Or Jefferson.

Islam recognizes that Allah chose Abraham, and covenanted first with the Hebrews. Islam recognizes Jesus was a prophet for change. In addition, Islam surely recognizes Allah's potential for fundamental change: the faith delivered by angels to the prophet Muhammad was itself a revolution. No less. But Islam, like its two sibling faiths, also believes the revelation it received 1,400 years ago was the final word.

Today, the world observes three children of the same father arguing that what father told them was his unchangeable last word. Experience teaches that a wise and loving father is more flexible. Indeed, God changed his mind many times in the Bible. Thus, change is everywhere in the life of Yahweh, the Lord, and Allah. Who can say that a benevolent Allah, seeing a better way for his faithful, would hide such a revelation because 1,400 years ago the Koran closed forever?

The Final Testament, if adopted by Islam as its newest book, would return Allah's children to an enlightened, tolerant, and progressive way, with full access to human potential. Islam had its golden epoch when such principles flowered. The *Final Testament*, combined with traditional Islamic teachings about community service and respect, can make it happen again. With Muslims gaining full participation in liberal self-governance, three words too often spoken in rote would become three words of ringing hope: "Allah be praised!"

Chapter Twenty-six

I nstitutional religion is by nature very conservative. Changes come slowly. Because its substance relies on the past, religion seems to be held hostage in antiquity's prison. Even more imprisoning is the instruction claimed by the three sibling faiths that theirs is the unchanging *last* word of the Lord. Logically, that cannot be. Surely, however, none will step forward and confess a misunderstanding of the one father's instructions. The Final Testament is an appropriate response, or perhaps rescue, from the binds of competing "true" faiths: all three children of God can together acknowledge the dynamic *new* word as the Father's revised guide to a just world.

The alternative to change is darkness. If religion keeps its scripture closed to renewal, it may suffer the quiet pain of irrelevance. In any event, the world is not well served in darkness, or when an important institution suffers ignominious irrelevance. The truth is always better. If the truth is not better, then religion is a poor teacher.

Rabbi Jesus spoke about truth to a group of very skeptical Jews, and his two-thousand-year-old words remain instructive:

> *[Y]ou will know the truth, and the truth will set you free. . . .*
> *I came from God and now I am here. I did not come on my own*
> *authority, but he sent me. Why do you not understand what I*
> *say? Is it because you cannot bear to listen to my message?*
> *(John 8:32, 42–43)*

The truth will set you free, although often it is very difficult to bear. Practice receiving it. Try to absorb God's words delivered 3,300 years ago by Moses to his warriors returning home with great numbers of prisoners:

Why have you kept all the women alive?... So now kill
every boy and kill every woman who has had sexual inter-
course, but keep alive for yourselves all the girls and women
who are virgins. (Num. 31:15–18)

This is profoundly disturbing. Kill every boy, and every woman who has had sexual intercourse. And God help the rest. Can we bear the implications of this Old Testament verse and what it says about God, at least when he was young?

Truth also means questioning scriptural beliefs. Are some of them legacies from a superstitious and tribal past? We may wonder, "Are Jews the chosen people?" They have consistently suffered more during the last 2,500 years than any group on earth. God or fate, it would seem, has been especially unkind to them.

Is faith in Jesus Christ the sole means to salvation in heaven? What a strange notion it is that the vast majority of people who have ever lived, or will ever live on this earth, are fated for eternal punishment by a loving God. Moreover, where is the fiery pit in which all the billions of unsaved souls are burning at this very moment?

Is Islam the final and superior revelation of the one God? Muslims say so, yet their societies around the world are almost without exception backward, impoverished, and unsuccessful by contemporary standards. The revelation seems not to be working.

Then there is the kind of illusion that brings to mind Arthur Miller's observation that "an era may be said to end when its basic illusions are exhausted." Surely, Jupiter, lord of the Roman world, fell victim to Miller's insight. However, today, we may consider the teaching by priests, rabbis, and imams that God is only good, just, and merciful. Facing the truth, we see that God's own autobiography confesses much that is ugly and worse. Once ancient scripture closed and the Lord ceased his recorded inspirations, additional unspeakable horrors continued unabated.

To take merely one example, but the worst one, we look at the Holocaust of World War II. Forty million people died because of that conflict. Among them were some six million Jews, of whom about one and a half million were children. Most of these Jewish victims were gassed or incinerated in ovens. Such a mass slaughter of civilian innocents is certainly history's most hideous carnage. What can we say of a loving and omnipotent God who watched but did nothing?

Since the Holocaust, there has been an endless stream of discussion dealing with the question *why*. Why did God let it happen? The answer, articulated a thousand different ways, comes down to this: we don't know. We don't know why during World War II, God failed to act, or why during the many other multimillion-person carnages, God failed to act. More simply, we don't know why God failed to save neighbor Ruth down the street from a terrible death from lung cancer. There is much we don't know.

God's perfection, it would seem, is an exhausted illusion. It should not come as a surprise that illusions going back millennia may falter in the face of new discoveries and sharper inquiry. However, imperfection does not require rejection. This is part of the good news of the Final Testament: we already have in our midst an updated and invigorating divine gift worthy of an imperfect God's redemption. Can we handle the truth? Yes, because we are not empty-handed and paralyzed, but recently gifted and empowered.

With truth in the matter, the ground is laid for a more honest, hopeful, and energetic faith. Courage will be needed, certainly, and to help muster it we can recall earlier Church history when rejecting change led to terrible consequences.

Although Jesus' listeners heard that the truth will set them free, the Church later decided otherwise. Thus began a long tradition of Christian intolerance for science and philosophy. The Church feared the truths derived from open inquiry. By contrast, the Greeks over centuries had invented and popularized scientific study of medicine, astronomy, mathematics, biology, and physics. In the realm of philosophy, Greek thinkers were revolutionaries in the fields of ethics and morality, political science, law, and drama.

All the world knows of Aristotle, Socrates, Plato, Pericles, Euclid, and the many other Greek contributors to the foundations

of Western civilization. Our Supreme Court and capitol build-
ings mimic Greek architecture because we praise by imitation the
continuum between classical Greek culture and our own hopes
for a cultured society. However, we do so with little thanks to the
Church because the Church was no friend of the truths that Greek
and then Roman thinkers sought to discover and popularize.

Greek-inspired inquiry was progressively unraveling the
secrets of the universe. However, the Church was wedded only to
the teachings of the Bible (i.e., the earth was flat, Adam and Eve
came first, demons and the devil take possession of bodies). Scientific learning was deemed a threat to fundamentalist theology,
and its proponents were persecuted. Even as late as 1610, Italy's
Galileo, who discovered and then used telescopes in an effort to
understand the structure of the universe, was publicly forced by
the Church to renounce his discoveries as heresy.

Sixteen hundred years after Jesus taught that truth would set
people free, the Church was still threatened by what it perceived
as the unraveling of the creation story, Adam and Eve, and other
set-in-stone doctrines. Threaten those foundations of faith, the
church warned the scientists, and you will burn here on earth for
a brief while and then in hell for an eternity. So much fire, but so
little light.

It is fascinating to speculate how differently the world may
have progressed if intellectual inquiry had not been held hostage
to the cross. If instead of fearing and obstructing scientific and
philosophical study from the 400s to the 1600s the Church had
urged such inquiries, the conclusions of a Newton, Descartes, or
Jefferson may have occurred hundreds of years earlier. Perhaps
the "dark ages"—a shutdown of learning—would never have
occurred.

It took the Protestant Reformation in the 1600s to set free
the truth that the truth does set us free. It took the American reformation in the 1700s to set free the truth that human beings must
be free. *By living free in all lands, humankind can finally be free
from mass evil.*

Should religion remain closed to the notion that God may want something better for a world enduring so much suffering? Closing religion in the past to new ideas was paid for with centuries of darkness. The resulting cost in lost progress and opportunity was enormous. Rather than limit scripture to the closed circles of ancient walled cities, why not run the risk for peace that God seems to be offering?

After all, can the pope declare with certainty that his Lord has nothing further to reveal and would never inspire the words of New World Protestants? Can Muslims rightly insist that Allah would never inspire English-speaking colonials in America? Can Jews accept there are many promised lands, and in all of them, the promise is dynamic freedom for all?

For more than one thousand years, the Church was afraid to consider that the world may be round. For twice that time, the Church has been afraid to consider that the world may *no longer* be under a sentence of apocalypse. Such resistance to change can only aid in the fulfillment of unhinged prophecy because darkness is a breeding ground for those who would do their worst.

The Church survived the discovery that the world is round, and it will happily survive the discovery that it is not ending. Therefore, rather than await apocalypse with the paralysis of "So it was written," why not consider that humankind possesses inalienable rights because God had it so written? Then the truth will set us free.

Some may ask, "Why should religion carry such a heavy burden of securing and protecting universal liberty?" Because there is no other way. Too much danger exists in the world for the slow processes of diplomacy, and much that passes for diplomacy is a genteel mechanism for ensuring the continuance of tyranny. How many brutal men have been wined and dined by gentlemen with elegant accents and devious agendas?

Regrettably, the world's leaders—even the most enlightened ones—tend toward coexistence with tyrants, and the results are tragic. Politicians are not in the virtue business. Therefore, people must lead, and then the leaders will follow. Such leadership is so important because the twenty-first century will be no different from the last one whenever and wherever tyrants rule. Where divine rights have been stolen, the resulting oppression breeds anger. From such places, the dangers are potentially too gruesome to ignore.

Cuba is a good example of a nation in need of the Final Testament. It is a beautiful and naturally rich island the size of Indiana. Eleven million people live under the dictatorship of Fidel Castro, who permits no one to earn more than $30 per month. All must work for the state; there is no private employment.

Now in its forty-sixth year of one man–no vote rule, the simple truth is that Castro was born of a mother and father like everyone else and with no greater right to dominate others than anyone reading this book. Fidel was a boy, then a bright young man, but along the way something occurred that in all eras remains a mystery. Like the biblical kings of God's warning, like Napoleon, Stalin, and Saddam Hussein, Castro developed the power lust and ruthlessness that insists upon domination of all others.

Such men kill, betray, imprison, and torture those who would prevent them from ruling. Thus, one dictator in military fatigues, aided by a circle of enablers, dictates to eleven million Cubans how they live, what they can do, and how impoverished they will be in their minds, hearts, and pockets. Why? To accommodate the despotic needs of one man, who in another time and place would be Pharaoh or Herod or Caesar. The Bible is filled with Castros, but the world doesn't need them.

Fortunately, the damage Castro causes is constrained by the modest size of his platform, a small island nation he has impoverished. However, technology has already made it possible for minor dictators to become major deliverers of havoc, thus greatly multiplying the danger.

The God of the New Testament, whose children in Cuba are or were faithful Catholics, has remained a quiet distance from his flock's suffering. The tragedy of the Catholic Church is that the Vatican has not daily reminded the world that Castro is a tyrant who ought to be removed. The Vatican's army of priests in Cuba and worldwide should in every church and parish raise their voices in a holy chorus against Castro's unholy oppression. Eleven million suffer from a local tyrant, but the father in Rome ignores the pain. Thus, religion in Cuba has virtually disappeared; the people's calls received only a busy signal, so they call no more.

Today, what more important mission could the Catholic Church have in Cuba than rescuing the faithful from despotism? Officiating at weddings and funerals is not enough when liberty is lost. Final Testament scripture would inform that inalienable rights—to speak, to travel, to write, to associate freely, and elect leaders—are divine and may not be squashed by Fidel Castro or those like him. With churches from Havana to Santiago in Cuba and others around the world reading Jefferson, insisting upon a Bill of Rights, and demanding free elections, a tidal wave for freedom would drown Castro. He would be gone. Sadly, forty-six years have already gone by. Why not a new beginning?

Another tragic example of the need for a new beginning is the Israeli/Palestinian conflict. Israel is a dynamic democracy. Palestine for decades was run by an authoritarian aligned with terrorists. There was no elected, effective legislature, and only now is there some stirring of freedom. Through decades of conflict, there was nothing like the checking and balancing of power that protects the people's ultimate sovereignty and collective voice. Suppose the Jewish and Muslim leaders of Israel and Palestine, as part of the broader canonization process, adopted the Declaration of Independence, the Constitution, and *The Federalist* as holy scripture. Suppose there was one scripture, under God, with liberty and justice for all. Suppose Palestine actually had a government of the people, for the people, and by the people, and it was supported by values that would keep it so.

Worth recalling is that Islam and Judaism coexisted one thousand years ago and could again today if enlightenment prevailed. If *both* Israel and Palestine functioned on the principle that their citizens have inalienable rights including life, liberty, and the pursuit of happiness, peace would follow. If the leaders failed to bring peace, new ones would be elected who would. Ordinary people wanting to lead normal lives would insist, and if empowered by their faith's scriptural liberties, they would insist in their synagogues and mosques until peace prevailed. Endless experience teaches what is already a cliché: democratic societies remain at peace unless attacked by others. What a wonderful cliché, for it was totally unknown in 1787 when no fully democratic states existed. Palestine should be added to the list of Final Testament faithful. Allah would approve.

The twentieth century was the classroom in which we all studied Evil 101. And 202, and 303. The biblical model of mayhem was in full tragic swing. Sadly, the biblical model of faith had little or no influence in diminishing the horror. However, the problems are not caused by ordinary people who farm, own shops, and do regular work while leading normal lives. Ordinary people do not wake in the morning and say, "Let's conquer and enslave our neighbors." In stark contrast are the malevolent souls, the men of God's "evil thoughts" description who are obsessed with power and domination of others. That is the lesson.

The hope? If Final Testament religion can finally put dynamic democracy in every house on the planet, we will indeed love our neighbors or, at the least, live quietly together.

Chapter Twenty-seven

I magine the oddity of a Baghdad newspaper in 2002 saying, "Hussein is a dictatorial murderer and has impoverished the soul and pockets of the country." It may sound funny, but the effect of denying free expression was the near enslavement of the Iraqi people. What should be the role of faith in Baghdad? To uplift spirits, empowering people to demand their right to life, liberty, and the pursuit of happiness. Surely, the tyrant would have been deposed by the Iraqis, and war avoided.

What if people everywhere could be energized by a belief that liberty is their inalienable right from Allah, or God by any other name? And the extraordinary thing is this: we already believe in our hearts that human rights are divine, and that Thomas Jefferson was right when in 1775 he wrote, "The God who gave us life gave us liberty at the same time."

Regrettably, suffering occurs not only in nations such as Syria and North Korea that are ruled by dictators. There is much quiet pain in seemingly democratic nations functioning imperfectly. Powerful people in such places have learned to manipulate circumstances to their advantage. Democracy does not turn bad men into angels. If successful, it controls their evil impulses, but where citizens are unmindful of their rights or threatened if they exercise them, the many may still be exploited by the few. Some leaders steal rights just as they steal less-sacred property.

In places like Latin America where religion is a powerful force, Final Testament congregations would be able to energize people by the millions to insist upon a more perfect union in which the Bill of Rights is sacred and respected. It is right for religion to teach in the world's dark corners that empowered democracy is the path to justice and equality. Many weak voices gathered together become irresistibly powerful, especially when divine energy is at work. Imperfect democracies will adjust in response. Corruption can be rooted out when and where it is no longer tolerated by congregations joined by faith in equality. Where despots rule, the rattles from thousands of mosques, temples, and churches will push them out because the purveyors of fear will themselves become the fearful.

Some may suggest the Final Testament is too difficult a text in areas of Latin America or Africa where education levels may be low. Of course, the same could be said of the Bible; it is no easy read. By comparison, the goals of the new scripture are clearer and closer to people's daily lives than mystical biblical generalities. The truths of the Federalist Papers are crisp and easy to grasp. Moreover, for one thousand years, the church denied people direct access to the Bible while clerics pruned and then preached its contents. By contrast, the Final Testament is directed toward personal empowerment, and its spirit is very accessible.

Experience also shows that in undeveloped nations, the collective wisdom and instincts of the uneducated citizenry are better guarantors of peace than the sophisticated oppression of the ruling few. The average citizen in the poorest land knows instinctively that peace and honest government mean decent meals and decent progress, while a strutting leader means trouble. Reining in bad leaders is truly a divine gift in such places. A university degree is unneeded for people to know when or if their bread will be buttered or even exist. We can be confident that enthusiastic individuals drawn to a ministry teaching the Bill of Rights will get the message across to the needy. The lessons of constitutional liberty will be the equal of an education, and education is power.

Of course, there will always be abusive leaders and reprehensible heads of state. People will not always get it perfect in their balloting because would-be rulers are apt to lie, lie often, and lie well. However, the worst will be turned out of office before they can do their worst. Such house cleaning by a free people requires the energetic exercise of meaningful rights. This process will be aided by the natural strength of aroused community voices generating hope. Hope is a wonderful return on invested faith.

If God was the father, then his tortured son on the cross was right to ask, "Why hast thou forsaken me?" We too have the right to ask that question regarding the endless wars, numbing tragedy, and murderous brutality through the centuries. However, there is an answer: the "forsaking" ended with the words "life, liberty, and the pursuit of happiness." From the quill of Thomas Jefferson in 1776, we surely have the briefest yet most powerful statement of what should be the goal of every nation for its citizens.

It is appropriate to wonder whether Final Testament scripture can respond to one's very personal needs. Often, we crave a God who will hear our prayers when a child becomes ill, a job is lost, or we can't find our house keys. Such hopes and yearnings will always arise, but can God be expected like a heavenly Santa Claus to daily minister to six billion people? Does he do that today? Moreover, new scripture does not mean a new Lord—only an invigorated, refreshed purpose for faith.

However, we can also envision the Final Testament as a celebration of the individual spirit. It recognizes an inner light of strength within all. The Founding Fathers did not sit by in the face of wrongs or in the midst of hardship. From a deep sense of personal commitment, many answered the call for personal action and personal sacrifice. The revolutionary effort was based on the idea that great accomplishment is possible despite the greatest odds. Fighting for freedom from the world's premier power in 1776 was a long shot. Rarely, however, will our individual burdens equal those faced by the Founding Fathers. They did so much with relatively little against great odds. So the Final Testament looks to the fight for freedom in this country as inspiration for the great personal effort often required in our own lives.

The most any heaven on earth can offer is freedom in a virtuous community and the chance to achieve our own great potential without hurting others. There will always be sickness, criminals, pain, losses, failure, drudgery, and emotional depression. Those things come with life, and a host of practices exist offering amelioration. On balance, however, mankind will surely benefit more if its many thousands of religious congregations worldwide clasp hands to fight the wholesale evil that imperils all. This too is reality. Without question, all faiths should be sensitive to the many varieties of individual suffering, but there are appropriate priorities in a very dangerous world where so many suffer collectively.

What better way could there be to meet each person's needs than to have a world in which every country, at peace, strives to implement the blessings of life, liberty, and the opportunity for the happiness of all citizens?

God's inspired books were cast in stone in ancient times. The priests doing the casting were surely the fundamentalists of their day who believed with ferocity every scriptural word they recognized as eternal. In those days, when material progress was imperceptible, eternal would cover an eternity. Traditional Jews would have foreseen sacrificing two lambs a day in the great temple for as long as stars cluttered the sky. In response, Christian radicals wanted to change the unchanging world in preparation for the end.

To grasp how ancient the eternal biblical era was, *imagine forward to the year 4500.* Yes, 4500, perhaps one hundred generations from today. What will *your family* be like then? It is just such an inconceivable block of time—in reverse—that takes us back to the religious leaders who proudly canonized this passage:

> *[W]hen you capture cities in the land that the Lord your God is giving you, kill everyone. (Deut. 20:16)*

Why would the priests canonize an order to kill so massively? No one knows, but it seems to have been the nature of the times; it was primitive tribal fundamentalism. In ancient Canaan, God's chosen were being given a Promised Land. The Lord wanted all the pagans dead so his people would have a religiously pure home. This command to massacre was, in that epoch and to those people, the just, merciful, and good blessing of a powerful Lord.

Depressingly, we can imagine certain of today's Islamic fundamentalists writing comparably horrific words as they seek to carry out their assertedly divine mission. All manner of vicious murder is employed in the task of purging the world for Islam. This unrestrained minority of religious extremists has, if we are open about this, a mindset gruesomely similar to that which carried out the slaughter of pagans in the name of the Lord of the Old Testament. Carnage is barbaric, whether Old Testament or new Islam. The tragedy is that today's fanatic Muslims echo the cries of seventh-century tribalism and religion. That is an ancient rut in which to be stuck.

It was the task of Jefferson and Madison to study the problems of time-entombed fundamentalism and then push mankind forward through revolutions of war and thought:

> *Had no important step been taken by the leaders of the Revolution for which a precedent could not be discovered . . . the people of the United States, might at this moment . . . have been laboring under the weight of some of those forms which have crushed the rest of mankind. (Federalist 68)*

God instructed that his word was never to change. Never. Yet, Christianity is the asserted changed word from Judaism. Islam is the asserted changed word from both. In writing the Constitution, the framers wrestled with the problem of whether to allow for change: should the document be cast in stone or be subject to amendment? The Bible was a precedent, and it was rejected. Wrote Madison:

> *A constitution devoid of a legal method of amendment can result in one of two alternatives: a static, unchanging political system, or change outside the constitutional order—by custom or by revolution. (Federalist 68)*

All faiths can escape the prison of the past by seeing the Lord as an active force for good, not just a mysterious invisible presence whom by rote we declare loving and merciful in a world evidencing too little of either virtue. Millions starve even today, especially in Africa, because leaders—callous authoritarians—treat their nations like personal opportunities, favor their sycophants, and disregard their citizens. In 2006, a holocaust continues in the Sudan.

It is quaintly insufficient in such places to fight hunger and holocaust with the message that Jesus volunteered to die on a Roman torture stake for *their* sins. Surely, God's modern message is that the non-elected and corrupt thugs running such countries should be retired. In the battle against evil, where else would God want to be? How refreshing it would be for the weak to experience their divine empowerment to be free and in control of their destiny.

Is it appropriate for religion to teach through scripture that non-elected oppressors have no place on this planet anymore, anywhere? Yes. What role could be more important in so many parts of the world for the future security and happiness of all people in all lands?

The faithful congregations—thousands of them—should sing the words of Jefferson and Madison and with raised voices be heard until their inalienable rights and better lives are restored. If inspired religion will lead, freedom will follow. Leaders and good people all around the world will pitch in to raise the barn where the people now starve.

Liberty is still young, merely a teenager in half of Europe. We already believe that liberty is the enemy of injustice. We know as well that revolution against political tyranny can be matched by our own personal revolution to be better, to do more, and to form a more perfect union with families, friends, and community. Congregations can speak to these issues and then do good things. The education of millions through these activities will result in many related benefits. People reading the Constitution and studying *The Federalist* will become valuable assets for their communities and nations. Ben Franklin's proverbs and the volumes of enlightened writings of the Founding Fathers are wonderful sources of wisdom for those seeking positive growth. Congregations will have endless opportunities for moral enrichment.

To some, it may seem strange to declare now, 230 years after the fact, that God divinely inspired Thomas Jefferson and his revolutionary colleagues. On the one hand, the events of that epoch seem so long ago, while at the same time they seem too familiar. Everyone knows Jefferson. Everyone knows Ben Franklin. George Washington is a national hero. They are part of the American cultural experience. Why divinity now? We have already observed that the books of the Jewish Bible were not instant bestsellers when first published millennia ago. Scripture may require centuries of seasoning. When the prophets Isaiah, Daniel, and Ezekiel spoke, their listeners could not then know that God had selected them for spreading his word. Perhaps they claimed such authority, and many may have believed it, but no one could be sure. Their words were canonized years later. Jesus? At the time of his death, even his disciples had abandoned him. He died virtually alone. Centuries passed before Jesus was widely accepted as a divine figure.

Change is a condition of existence. Can we consider that God, too, may grow and change, inspiring new teachings in the process? The Final Testament is providential because the urgency to fully implement the gift is great. Technology has so broadened the opportunity for mass destruction by the few, that the many cannot be patient with the current pace of liberty's spread. The clock is ticking. The goal is universal peace—a first—and its foreseeable possibility is why the greatest event in two thousand years was the American Revelation.

In the end, it is a matter of faith whether there was divine intervention two millennia ago or two centuries ago. However, faith should be given only after we feel confident that truth has been given a chance, and that fear is not the driver. That the world may be saved as a result is good reason to have faith.

Chapter Twenty-eight

New Scripture and Divine Intervention

The Final Testament is a call for a renewed faith in response to the seemingly miraculous. Of course, some will say that monotheism is perfectly fine as it is. "Thank you, but no changes are needed." History teaches, however, that with faith, you renew it or lose it. Hundreds, or perhaps even thousands, of deities once held court among clans, tribes, and nations across the earth. Now they are footnotes in history books.

"Eternal" Jupiter reigned for 1,000 years. Today, only tourists visit his temples. In his glory days Rome's supreme god had dramatically and passionately ruled the heavens from England to India. Then, in AD 327, King Constantine made a pact with Christianity, and soon Jupiter was no more. Surely many Romans felt deep pain at the passing of their eternal god.

We can imagine a gathering of faithful at the temple of Jupiter Optimus Maximus on Rome's Capitoline Hill, beautifully sited above the regal city. Honeysuckled breezes float through vapors of gloom as Zeusteres, the old leader of a proud Roman legion, stands with his soldiers one last time.

My dear Jupiter, your faithful gather here in your house with grief beyond measure. You have blessed us so. As for me, ninety-five summers mark my time in this world. Now, my ancient limbs shake with despair at what some say is your passing.

When I was a boy in Rome, my father Hertemes told me of your powers, your triumphs and victories. Our beautiful Rome received your wisdom and welcomed your guiding hand. Our warriors won victory after victory with the strength you placed in our hearts. You were my miraculous God on blood-soaked battlefields stretching to Persia. And in my tent at night, your muses inspired special verses shared with homesick comrades. However, thoughts of your beautiful daughters Diana and Minerva helped us recall the beauty of our beloved Rome, no matter how dark the night or fearsome the enemy.

My dear Jupiter, our King Constantine now prays to another god. The Christians with whom he has allied cursed you as pagan statuary. Marble signifying nothing. The Jews say you never were. They are wrong. In my long life, I have sent you prayers and praise, and even the broken bodies of my brave soldiers. You returned to me gifts of hope, children, victory, and years of life. More than I deserve. Now they say you are no more. During our march across half the world, I have seen a thousand gods, and all fell before your power. Strange gods of every shape and bent were crushed to dust by our swords, and then the people there came to love you as their own. Even the Jews, with their almighty invisible god who created the universe in seven days—so they proudly claim—fell like pebbles before you.

It cannot be that you are "no more." I am a soldier. I have lived for war and found peace in knowing of your love for our people. You have given us everything. The world honors your inspired victories and gifts in law, science, philosophy, literature, and civilization. No other god has so blessed his children. I am filled with tears. There cannot be such emptiness as a world without eternal Jupiter. Where would you go? How could I find you there? It is for others to bid you farewell, for I do not understand abandonment. It is not the way of an old soldier. You are the mightiest God, and I shall stay with you, always.

How despairing it must have felt to learn that Jupiter and his family of gods had been replaced. Replaced? Does that mean one thousand years of prayers had been in vain? A lie? That the eternal supreme deity known to Rome as Jupiter and to Greece as Zeus *never existed*? Were all the bright people of Greece and Rome living for one thousand years at the epicenter of knowledge, praying to nonexistent gods? *Were they all fooled?*

The irony is sharp: Romans and Greeks achieved unparalleled success in war, commerce, and culture while praying in temples *named* for gods but apparently containing none. Meanwhile, the chosen were continually conquered and dispersed while praying to the real God. The wealth of the world had flowed to the Greeks and the Romans; the wrath of the world flowed to the Jews. Surely, this mismatch in blessings and rewards contributed to the "end of the world" syndrome preached by traditional Jews, and then adopted by the revolutionary Jewish sect known as Christians. How upside down it all was.

Despite the extraordinary successes of Greece and Rome, the gods of those empires fell from heaven after a thousand-year reign. They had been contemporaries of the biblical Lord. However, faith in Jupiter and his extended family of deities began to wither until somewhere in the ancient world the very last believer finally said, "No more." Now, as with the sound of a tree falling in the forest we may ask, "Did they ever exist?"

The lesson is clear: the death of mighty Jupiter shows that even eternal gods are not immortal. We should do what we can to render irrelevant the question, did God ever exist? Perhaps we can do that by answering the question, did God intervene in 1776?

Chapter Twenty-nine

Congress on Canonization

I t is time to return to historic Independence Hall in Philadelphia and begin the next revolution. The Congress on Canonization should commence. From that hallowed hall, people across the world should hear the words that all men are endowed by their Creator with inalienable rights which the powerful, the lucky, the tyrannical, or the purely evil cannot steal or diminish.

Can the Declaration of Independence, the Constitution of the United States, and *The Federalist* actually be canonized as scripture? If there is faith, then absolutely. The Congress should be composed of the world's wisest religious leaders from Islam, Christianity, and Judaism. They would be assisted by university presidents, esteemed scholars, historians, sociologists, and others whose unquestioned wisdom and maturity would command international respect. No politicians or elected officials need apply since canonization is a private religious affair, totally separate from the state.

These men and women would have a profound responsibility. They would be deciding issues likely to alter history, affect billions of people, and prove that good can defeat evil. The Congress would consider whether the three proposed documents were divinely inspired and therefore reflect the teaching of God. The religious leaders would also determine if their faiths will recognize as new scripture for their prayer books and congregational use the Declaration of Independence, the Constitution of the United States, and *The Federalist*.

Consider the unique deliberations. Was there divine intervention during the years 1776–1791 in establishing freedom and the processes that secure it? The Congress' work would generate extraordinary worldwide interest via cable news and other media coverage. In cities and villages all over the earth, from Pakistan to Haiti, Malaysia or Senegal, people would follow the proceedings and be caught up in the discussion. All would have opinions on whether the ancient scriptural God came forward in 1776 to reveal a revolutionary way to tame evil and generate peace. All would wonder: did a divine hand move men in the New World to make a new world? Was God liberated from the Near East to liberate men everywhere?

Worldwide, people would read copies of the Declaration of Independence, the Constitution, histories of the Revolutionary era, and *The Federalist*. Can liberty be divine? One can imagine debates in classrooms, cafés, and Kasbahs. People would want to know if a divine grace ran through Thomas Jefferson. How can we make freedom work better, or, as the case may be, why does our non-elected leader deny us our inalienable rights?

The interconnected planet would see and hear the testimony of the world's best minds and hearts, live from Independence Hall in Philadelphia, reviewing scripture, world history, the meaning of faith, the madness of evil, and the nature of freedom, man, and God. There would be a once-in-a-millennium search for the truth through every path of inquiry. Did God move Thomas Jefferson's quill to write that all men are created equal? Did the Lord's light open Madison's eyes to unique ways of taming the beast of evil? Were *The Federalist* essays providential teachings delivered so that the architecture of constitutional liberty can be secured everywhere with the necessary explanations?

Let the questions and debates fly. The media will note how the non-elected leaders squirm as their people learn of democracy's birth and its destiny in their oppressed lands. The power of freedom's pull will be irresistible. Values and virtues will add lift to the process. Finally, in a world of free people exercising their inalienable rights, Isaiah's most important prophecy may yet come true:

They will hammer their swords into plows and their spears into pruning knives. Nations will never again go to war, never prepare for battle again. (Isa. 2:4)

Thomas Jefferson was a lifelong progressive. He recognized the need for change. He advocated a good and healthy political housecleaning every twenty years because "institutions must advance and keep pace with the times."

Some men look at constitutions with sanctimonious reverence, and deem them like the Ark of the Covenant, too sacred to be touched. They ascribe to the men of a preceding age a wisdom more than human . . . But I know also that . . . as new discoveries are made, new truths disclosed, and manners and opinions change with the circumstances, institutions must advance also and keep pace with the times.

If renewal every twenty years is considered too frequent, then certainly every two thousand years allows sufficient time for new truths to emerge that may provide better guidance.

Our founders' good works have contributed more in 230 years to the causes of justice, freedom, human progress, and the fight against mass evil than anyone or anything since the last divine covenant. Certainly, that is a contentious claim, and many may disagree. Nevertheless, let the Congress on Canonization begin. *Divine intervention?*

Let truth and liberty win out over fear, for we who are free today have been blessed like none in the Holy Bible could imagine.

Not the end, but the beginning

Thank You

Dear Reader,

Thank you for reading *Divine Intervention: Jesus or Jefferson?* [DI] I hope your journey through these pages has been as enlightening and inspirational for you as the research and writing process was for me.

If you enjoyed my work I recommend the sequel, an adventure/romance novel entitled *Romancing the Bible*. It is a rollercoaster thriller as writer Jared Kimmel flees from assassins desperate to prevent DI from being published. The break-neck action, romance, and humor form a unique platform upon which to present DI's provocative themes as the drama hurtles along from Los Angeles through Latin America. I feel confident *Romancing the Bible* will leave you happily breathless *and* enlightened. But fair warning: an active intellectual curiosity, sense of humor, and belief in love are prerequisites for a proper read. You are invited to learn more at RomancingTheBible.com.

And so dear reader, whatever path you travel in this extraordinary process called life, I hope your journey will draw inspiration from *Divine Intervention*.

Sincerely,

Stanley Kimmel Kesselman

Author's Note
and Acknowledgment

My life changed when I read these Old Testament words:

Every living being on the earth died—every bird, every animal, and every person. Everything on earth that breathed died.

It was the first holocaust, recorded in Genesis, following the Great Flood.

And these words:

If two men are having a fight and the wife of one tries to help her husband by grabbing hold of the other man's genitals, show her no mercy; cut off her hand.

One of the ancient Lord's 613 commandments until the end of time.

And finally, this flight into numbing darkness:

However, if you do not obey the Lord your God and do not carefully follow all his commands and decrees . . . you will be hungry, thirsty, and naked—in need of everything. The Lord will oppress you harshly until you are destroyed. . . . The Lord will plague you with diseases until he has destroyed you from the land. . . . The Lord will strike you with wasting disease, with fever and inflammation, with scorching heat and drought . . . until you perish. . . . The Lord will turn the rain of your country into dust and powder. . . until you are destroyed. The Lord will inflict you with the boils of Egypt and with tumors and festering sores . . . and with madness, blindness, and confusion of mind.

Divine threats far beyond comprehension; then, carried out.

From these verses and others, I developed an aching need to discover a better path for a better Lord. The search led through countless sources of all descriptions. Often, I hastily made notes or collected quotes. Not having any specific purpose in mind, my jottings lacked citations or reference.

Thus, my apology. This is a nonacademic work intended as a beginning point for readers courageous enough to travel a new path. It relies most heavily on the Good News Bible, Today's English Version. If there are uncited quotations from other sources, my regrets to these authors that time and circumstance have colluded in omissions of attribution. In turn, readers are welcome to borrow brief quotations from my work. My goal is to spread the good news of a better way.

A genuine thank you goes to an array of gifted writers who have inspired me—pro or con—and to whose excellent works I invite my readers for further inquiry:

Rescuing the Bible , John Shelby Spong
Myths of the Bible, Gary Greenberg
The Harlot by the Side of the Road, Jonathan Kirsch
The New Revelations, Neale Donald Walsch
Deceptions and Myths of the Bible, Lloyd M. Graham
The Genesis of Justice, Alan M. Dershowitz
Wide as the Waters, Benson Bobrick
The Federalist, edited by Benjamin F. Wright
On Two Wings, Michael Novak
The Good Book, Peter J. Gomes
James Madison, Ralph Ketcham
The Book of God, Walter Wangerin Jr.
John Adams, David McCullough
The Bible and the Ancient Near East, Cyrus Gordon and Gary
    Rendsburg
Who Wrote the Bible? Richard Elliott Friedman
From Jesus to Christ, Paula Fredriksen
A History of God, Karen Armstrong

The Case for Faith, Lee Strobol
Jefferson Himself, edited by Bernard Mayo
The Jefferson Bible, Thomas Jefferson
The Religions of Man, Huston Smith
The American Soul, Jacob Needleman

Former Bishop John Shelby Spong deserves special mention because his writings are not only uniquely creative, but his courageous departure into unorthodoxy inspired me to stretch far beyond the comfortable. However, I sincerely thank all of these writers for educating me, challenging me, and contributing immensely to our understanding of biblical and key historical events.

And to Jesus and Jefferson, my profound respect and love.

Stanley Kimmel Kesselman,
Los Angeles, California, 2006